100 Ways
to Cut the
High Cost of
Attending College

100 Ways to Cut the High Cost of Attending College

MONEY-SAVING ADVICE FOR STUDENTS AND PARENTS

Michael P. Viollt

Cooper Square Press

Published by Cooper Square Press
A Member of the Rowman & Littlefield Publishing Group
200 Park Avenue South, Suite 1109
New York, New York 10003-1503

Distributed by National Book Network

Library of Congress Cataloging-in-Publication Data

Viollt, Michael P., 1951–
     100 ways to cut the high cost of attending college : money-saving
     advice for students and parents / Michael P. Viollt.
          p. cm.
     Includes bibliographical references.
     ISBN 0-8154-1203-7 (paper : alk. paper)
          1. Student aid—United States. 2. College students—United
     States—Finance, Personal. I. Title: One hundred ways to cut the high
     cost of attending college. II. Title.

     LB2337.4 .V56 2002
     379.3—dc21

                                                            2002001046

Contents

Acknowledgment

One of the great strengths of America is its rich and diverse system of higher education. Collectively the colleges and universities of this system make a college education attainable for just about everyone. This equal opportunity for quality education is the envy of every other nation on the planet. All of the other countries of the world understand that education is the foundation of prosperity and the great equalizer of all mankind.

This formula for national success is based upon the assumption that we can continue to provide affordable college options to all prospective students. I hope this book will help my daughters Anne and Sarah, their friends, and an entire generation find the college that best meets their needs. All who use this book to that end owe a great deal of gratitude to Petra and Meagan for their valuable insight and assistance with the production of this work.

Introduction

Most students report that their number one concern regarding college is affordability. They have good reason for concern, considering that the cost of college continues to increase at twice the rate of inflation. This annual cost spiral has many families and individuals wondering if they will be able to pay for a college education.

College costs are a much larger percent of family income than they were just ten years ago. During the 1990s, median family income rose 38 percent while college tuition went up nearly 60 percent and 80 percent at private and public colleges respectively. For high school graduates and adults going to college, these tuition increases have made attaining a degree a very expensive proposition. Cost is the number one reason that less than half of all college students graduate. But cost need not keep you from earning a degree. As you select a college, remember that you can find quality in every price range. You can spend $200,000 for a college education or $11,000, and often get the same return on your investment as measured by lifetime earnings or more qualitatively by things such as lifestyle, friendships made, and personal development. The trick is to find the right fit for you.

Tuition prices offer just one measure of the cost of higher education. Actual cost is impacted by the amount of financial help you receive, the number of terms you are enrolled, the educational value you receive, and the overall return on your investment. After considering tuition and fees, the largest variable in college cost is the amount of financial aid that you receive from outside sources and the financial aid (discount) offered to you by the college or university. In a college class of twenty students, every one of them may pay a different tuition rate after including scholarships and grants (discounts). Tuition rates often have little to do with the underlying cost of delivering the education. In this way, they work similar to the price tag on perfume, where the basic ingredients are the same in all perfumes but prices vary greatly based upon the status position of the product. The "price" of a college is often set to align the college with other schools in a certain class. Colleges have a perceived value that may or may not reflect the true quality of the education. Other variances in tuition can hinge on the amount of tax support a college receives, the size of the college's endowment fund (savings), its location, the amount of research conducted at the college, faculty teaching load and a number of other factors.

Financial assistance comes from a large number of sources, and for many students, this aid determines where they can go to college. About three-fourths of all students receive financial aid. Most, about 80 percent of the aid, comes from government sources, while most of the remainder comes from the schools themselves. For the average student, aid covers about 40 percent of college costs. This aid is broken into 40 percent grants and 60 percent loans. The loans will have to be paid back with interest. The grants are not paid back.

Even with financial aid, most families will be stretched to meet college costs. As with anything else of value in life, you will have to make sacrifices to earn your degree. You need to decide in advance what trade-offs you are willing to make in your quest to keep college affordable. Which of your "important" college selection criteria are you willing to give up?

As the cost of an education increases, you are forced to look at college as an investment. When you consider that even after discounts and other sources of help, the average student graduates with $18,000 in debt, it is no wonder that students want to get the most out of every dollar.

You can achieve the "softer" college results—maturing, friendship development, group activities, special-interest development, value creation, etc.—at just about any college. For most students, the "right fit" is the college that provides for most of their education and experience wants, yields solid career results, and is affordable.

You can succeed in life without a college education—it is just a lot harder to do. College is available and affordable for just about everyone. Take the time to find the college that best fits your needs and you will have made an affordable choice. I hope this book will help you do that.

CHAPTER 1

The Three Elements of College Affordability

I t is true that there is more to selecting a college than dollars and cents, but affordability is the most critical concern for most college students. The 100 cost-saving strategies in this book will help you make the most of your "college dollar." The strategies fall into three basic categories: lowering the price of tuition and fees, maximizing the value received for your investment, and increasing the amount of money you receive from other sources. Before you begin to investigate the 100 tips, spend a little time learning how the three categories work together to impact affordability. It will help you in your planning to understand why there is such great variability in the cost of an education.

College Costs

The cost of a college education represents both your immediate out-of-pocket expenses for things such as tuition, fees, books, and supplies, and the number of terms of study you need to earn your degree. It is much easier to control for terms of study needed to graduate then it is to control price. Time to graduation varies greatly from student to student, even at the same college. It is both the difference in time and price that results in the wide range of total student costs.

LIST PRICE – Tuition, fees, books, and living costs.

In the 2002-2003 school year annual tuition will average $2000 at community colleges, $4,000 at public universities, and $18,000 at private colleges/universities. The price of tuition and fees at a college depends on a mix of pricing strategies that the college employs. Sometimes schools will use just one of these strategies to set tuition, while at other times they'll rely on a combination of factors. Colleges often set their tuition rate based on what people are willing to pay. Schools in a particular group of similar institutions compete with each other for students, and these students set the price, so to speak, through their selection process. Colleges that have many more applicants than seats available will often begin raising tuition rates.

In an attempt to create a certain image, tuition is often set merely to align a college with other similar schools. These schools base their pricing on the idea that students will judge a college based on the company it keeps. There thinking is, "If it's expensive, it must be good."

The most basic form of tuition pricing is to simply pass on the real cost of educating a student. This strategy is more likely found at institutions with high fees that differ for each program offered. In other words, an engineering student may pay more than a student in the sociology department. This practice is similar to pricing found in construction; the customer is billed for time and materials, plus an increment for profit, or in the case of colleges—surplus funds.

Some colleges will adjust their tuition to capture any increase in financial aid announced by government sources. If federal or state aid increases, these schools raise tuition by a similar amount. This allows colleges to keep students' out-of-pocket expenses constant while increasing the college's revenue.

Whatever strategy a college uses to set its tuition rate, you should know that some rates are justified and others are not. The strategies presented in this book will help you find a college that will provide you with a quality education at a price you can afford.

TIME TO GRADUATION – The number of semesters/ quarters needed to earn a degree.

Colleges don't design ways to keep you in school longer. However, they do promote policies and practices that, in effect, hinder you from graduating in a timely way. These practices include everything from poor academic planning to indifference to your needs.

For some faculty, advising students is a distraction. These instructors may be less than helpful in the course planning process. Full-time staff counselors often have caseloads too large to manage, making it impossible for them to spend quality time with students. Good faculty advising can help students plan their optimum schedule, while a lack of good advice can result in miscues that cause longer than desired college stays. Conflicting job responsibilities can compromise the quality of advising. At many colleges faculty concentrate on research rather than students. Some of these professors will see students, particularly undergraduates, as interfering with their research and writing.

The higher-level courses upperclassmen need to meet graduation requirements fill up fast. These courses are often taught by top faculty in the department who can only handle so many classes, limiting the number of students who can take the course in a given term. Some schools have little concern for getting more sections added to meet student demand. This lack of course availability contributes to scheduling problems.

Federal financial-aid programs, as well as most state and college-based grant programs, do not provide aid on a year-round basis. They simply run out of available aid and must wait for a new year to begin to replenish the scholarship and grant budgets. These arbitrary rules penalize diligent students who want to go to school year-round. Most aid practices are not designed for timely graduation.

By following the tips presented in this book, you can dramatically cut your time to degree and hence, the total cost of your degree. You have more control over this cost variable, time to degree, than any other.

Money from Others

You and your family should expect to pay for your college education, but a big share of most students' educational expenses actually comes from other sources. These sources include government agencies, employers, sponsors, and the colleges themselves. These funds take the form of scholarships, grants, loans, tax-breaks, pay for service, and investment returns. Most importantly, they also include the aid a college will give you in the form of a discount to tuition, commonly referred to as a grant or scholarship.

SCHOLARSHIPS, GRANTS, AND OTHER FINANCIAL AID

Tuition discounts create the greatest difference in what one student pays over another for college. Schools use discounts to achieve a number of different goals, usually related to attracting a certain type of student. There are many reasons for discounting tuition (offering scholarships/grants); a basic understanding of some of them will help in your college selection process.

Many colleges simply offer certain discounts because they have done so in the past. Often, these programs were established by an outside gift and must remain in place for long periods of time. These scholarships or grants are usually well publicized and easy for you to identify.

Colleges increasingly follow the model of airlines and fill seats in incoming classes by offering differing aid packages. They will develop different discounts (grants) based on the students' time of application and desired academic program. Some schools will offer steep discounts in some majors while offering none in other subject areas.

Most colleges will give a larger discount to students who match an institutionally attractive profile. Students with special talents and academic abilities will benefit from these awards. In turn, these students enhance the college's image.

The more you understand about a particular college's "discounting" policy, the better your chances are of getting institutional financial aid. Scholarships and grants awarded directly from the college are just one small part of the total financial aid available. The majority of aid packages include grants and loans from both federal and state government agencies. Knowing how to get all of the aid you are entitled to will go a long way toward making college affordable.

SAVINGS AND TAX BREAKS

An educated citizenry is a great benefit to a country. This is one reason that local, state, and national programs have been established to assist you in paying for your college education. These assistance programs take the form of educational saving/investment incentives and tax breaks.

The combination of incentives and tax breaks offered can seem complicated and at times redundant. By carefully planning for a college education, you and your family can find huge savings through these programs.

OTHER SOURCES OF COLLEGE FUNDS

There are many organizations that will help with your college expenses if you are wiling to give something in return. The trick is to find a service function that is of interest to you and that pays for college. You may decide to work, volunteer, or even join the armed forces to fund your education. It is best if you do these things for other reasons and secondarily enjoy the tuition assistance benefits. Self-help has always been the best way to get ahead. You can gain experience and college funds.

Total Return

The return on investment section is the least tangible but probably the most important component of college planning. It is simply a measure of what you get in exchange for your money, time, and effort. Your return on investment relates both to the immediate quality of education and the long-term benefits that you realize over a lifetime. Viewed from this vantage point, college is like any other purchase you make—if you are not careful you may not get a good value.

A college education represents a huge investment; often one of the largest you will make in your lifetime. You need to measure the return your education pays over time, in comparison to alternate investments that you could be making.

QUALITY OF EDUCATION – Are you getting what you pay for?

You will probably find educational value fairly subjective. Even the experts have trouble quantitatively evaluating it. A recent national study evaluated higher education in each state and could not compare states on educational value because educators across the country could not agree on what should be taught in college. Some institutions use this lack of consensus on indicators of quality to their advantage and do whatever they want. Others look for what students want and attempt to deliver that. In the end, the marketplace of employers, graduate schools, and community members will decide the true value of a particular college degree.

There are some basics that most can agree upon. The majority of students and most employers want degrees to lead to a career, or at least offer some sort of practical application. At a certain level, all education is applied to something. But not all schooling is applied to a related job, profession, or graduate program.

If the quality of your education is poor, then you wasted your money, no matter how high or low the price of tuition. This book will give you ways to identify strong academic programs and point out potential pitfalls you may find in your search for educational value.

LONG-TERM BENEFITS—What are you prepared to do at graduation?

College does more than prepare students for careers, and careers are selected for reasons other than what your college major was. However the majority of students consider career development the number one reason why they enrolled in college. Unfortunately, all degrees do not provide the desired career launching pad. Many majors do little to prepare you for today's world of work. Some college majors should come with a surgeon general type of warning— "THIS PROGRAM MAY NOT LEAD TO A JOB AT GRADUATION."

Students and parents often are surprised when graduates encounter a tough job market in their major field. They report that college did little to help them prepare for work in their field of study. Surprisingly, many graduates are shocked to learn that they need additional education just to land a job. It is our experience that more than 80 percent of the job offers go to college graduates in just 20 percent of the fields of study.

If you get nothing else from college, at least ensure that you learn the skills you need to pursue your career dreams.

CHAPTER 2

Making Trade-Offs

What Is Most Important to You in College Planning?

Like all of life's major endeavors, college planning requires trade-offs. While we all would like to find our ideal situation, we usually settle for something less. It is important to concentrate on getting what you consider truly essential or critical in college planning and to give up on things that you view as being less important. For instance, some students want to attend a top-name college. They want to wear the name of the school on T-shirts and display it on their car window. Other students don't care about national reputation and simply want good results at an affordable price.

The items listed below represent outcomes that you can expect to achieve by using this book. Review them and rank the item most critical in your college planning process as a 10. The second most important one gets a 9, the third 8, and so on. When you finish, go on to the next page for an explanation of how to use these results.

Getting The Most Reputation You Can	☐	Earning A Degree As Fast As Possible	☐
Finding Affordable Tuition	☐	Finding Ways To Keep College-Related Costs Down	☐
Balancing College With Current Commitments	☐	Maximizing Available Financial Aid	☐
Training For A Job	☐	Saving For College Attendance In The Future	☐
Building Career Potential	☐		
		Getting The Best Education You Can	☐

Which of the 100 Strategies Will Best Serve You?

The table on the next page will help you determine which of the 100 strategies presented in this book will provide you with the best opportunities for managing your college costs. Place your ranked scores from the above in the boxes on the next page for each of the corresponding items.

Then begin by reviewing your highest-ranking criteria. Review the tips that correspond to that item. These are the strategies that present the best use of your educational dollar. You can then work your way down your list from those ranked 10, 9, etc. The lower your rank score, the less you are gaining by following the corresponding tips. These lower ranked outcomes are the ones that are best given up as a compromise in your college planning.

	Tips
☐ Getting the Most Reputation You Can	84-89
☐ Finding Affordable Tuition	1-9, 30-45
☐ Balancing College with Other Commitments	55-67
☐ Training for a Job	90-95
☐ Building Career Potential	96-100
☐ Earning a Degree as Fast as Possible	18-29
☐ Finding Ways to Keep College Related Costs Down	10-18
☐ Maximizing Available Financial Aid	18-29, 30-45
☐ Saving for College Attendance in the Future	46-54
☐ Getting the Best Education You Can	68-89

CHAPTER 3

Look for Lowest List Prices

The strategies in this section will help you save on basic college expenses. They offer saving tips on items such as tuition, fees, books, and living expenses. You will find that you need not sacrifice value to gain affordability.

1. Attend a Community College

Community Colleges are not for losers. One of the best ways to save on a college education is to use the community college as a starting point. Many students begin their education at a community college and then transfer to a four-year institution (senior college) after one or two years of study. Next year, over 50 percent of all college students will be enrolled at a community college. No other education option delivers such a strong combination of quality instruction and reasonable costs.

Stat-to-Know

You can save $30,000–$50,000 in college costs by beginning your education at the local community college.

In fact, for your first two years of study, a community college can provide a better education than you might receive at a large university. Faculty members at community colleges are well educated, have appropriate credentials, and focus on teaching rather than research. By comparison, at a large public university, students may find that up to half of their courses during the first two years are taught by graduate teaching assistants. These assistants are typically not career educators.

When doing your course planning, don't feel that you must work toward an associate's degree at a community college. If you plan to continue on at a four-year school, take courses that will fit your intended baccalaureate field of study (Cost-Saving Strategy 20). After you transfer and finish your degree, few people will care where you spent your first year or two of college, they will be more concerned about where you earned your bachelor's degree. If they ask about your years at a community college, they will likely be impressed with your strategy and its related savings. Even when compared with a public university, the cost of attending a community college will be 50 to 70 percent less.

Remember that a community college is not a college of last resort. Don't be pressured by classmates that put down community colleges. Investigate them for yourself. They are conveniently located and charge very low tuition. Many students find community colleges an excellent choice for their freshman and sophomore years. Beginning a four-year degree at a community college will become the preferred choice for the majority of students in the near future.

INSIDER'S ADVICE

WHAT SHOULD YOU TAKE AT A COMMUNITY COLLEGE?

LOAD UP ON	AVOID
▶ Math	▶ Vocational course work, i.e., horticulture, radiology, etc.
▶ English – composition, research, analysis	
▶ Introductory courses – in the sciences and social sciences	▶ Advanced-level course work, i.e., intermediate accounting, operations management
▶ Courses in areas you will need some special assistance	▶ Specialized electives – photography, animation
▶ General electives – art, music	▶ More than three courses in any field
▶ Basic computer technology	▶ Pursuing a degree at the community college
▶ Courses identified as transferable by your choice of senior institutions	▶ Non-credit courses
▶ A foreign language sequence	▶ Independent study
	▶ Life experience credit
	▶ Distance learning courses
	▶ Shortened time frame courses
	▶ Interdisciplinary courses

2. Study Tuition Increase Patterns

Avoid colleges that have had unusually large tuition increases in recent years. The old rule that the best way to predict future performance is by reviewing past performance holds true when evaluating colleges. It is difficult enough to pay this year's tuition without playing the guessing game of what next year's tuition increase might be. In recent years, colleges have done everything from decreasing tuition to increasing it by more than 18 percent. This can make it difficult for students and their families to plan for the resources they will need to meet next year's tuition.

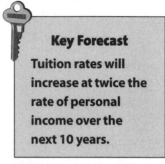

Key Forecast

Tuition rates will increase at twice the rate of personal income over the next 10 years.

When evaluating a college, it is important to review the school's pattern of tuition increases, since most colleges tend to have similar increases from one year to the next. Admission counselors or recent guide books can give you this information. Be sure to ask about any unusually high increases that seem out of historical character for a college. Sometimes a school increases tuition in one specific year to bring it closer to similar institutions. In that case, it does not mean tuition will continue to be raised at that rate.

You may be pleasantly surprised to find some colleges have had no recent tuition increases because of their commitment to keeping tuition affordable for as many students as possible. Community colleges, in particular, have been leaders in finding ways to hold their tuition down, providing opportunities for everyone to attend college (Cost-Saving Strategy 1).

THE WINNERS

COLLEGES WITH A HISTORY OF SMALL TUITION INCREASES

State	University
Alabama	Alabama State University
	Selma University
	Stillman College
	University of South Alabama
	University of West Alabama
Arizona	University of Phoenix
Arkansas	Southern Arkansas University Tech
California	California State University-Fresno
	California State University-Fullerton
	California State University-Northridge
	Humboldt State University
	Lincoln University
District of Columbia	Southeastern University
Illinois	Chicago State University
	National-Louis University
	Robert Morris College
Louisiana	University of Louisiana-Monroe
Massachusetts	University of Massachusetts
Mississippi	Mississippi State University
	Mississippi Valley State University
	Northwest Mississippi State University
	University of Mississippi

(Continued)

COLLEGES WITH A HISTORY OF SMALL TUITION INCREASES (Continued)	
Montana	Montana State University
Nebraska	Grace University
New York	CUNY (all branches)
	SUNY (all branches)
Ohio	Ohio State University
	Ohio University
	University of Cincinnati
Oklahoma	Carl Albert State University
	East Central University
	Northeastern State University
	Northwestern Oklahoma State University
	Southwestern Oklahoma State University
Texas	University of Mary Hardin Baylor
Virginia	Liberty University

3. Compare Tuition Rates

Just because a college charges higher tuition, doesn't mean it offers a better education. Colleges and universities can be placed into six broad categories for comparison purposes. Each group contains a large number of schools that offer a range of tuition rates. When selecting a college, you will want to compare the average tuition rate after discounts with other schools in the same classification. While two colleges from different classifications may have very similar tuition rates, you need to avoid making comparisons across classification types (categories). Cost comparing schools from different categories would be similar to comparing the cost of SUV's with that of sedans. If you have not selected the type of college you want cost is a poor way to select a category. Within each category you will find affordable choices and a number of expensive choices.

CHECKLIST

THE SIX CATEGORIES OF COLLEGES AND UNIVERSITIES

▶ Large Public Research Universities

▶ Private Research Universities

▶ Smaller Colleges/Universities focused on professional fields

▶ Liberal Arts Colleges

▶ Private Specialty Schools (Bachelor's Level) - offering only specialty fields.

▶ Community Colleges (Associate's Level)

While tuition can vary greatly among colleges in a single category, there is a basic relationship between category type and average tuition rates. In simplest form, the higher degree level offered in a sector (public or private) the higher the tuition rate. The private colleges in general charge a higher rate than publicly-supported institutions.

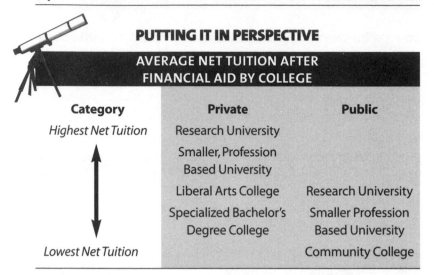

Category	Private	Public
Highest Net Tuition	Research University	
	Smaller, Profession Based University	
	Liberal Arts College	Research University
	Specialized Bachelor's Degree College	Smaller Profession Based University
Lowest Net Tuition		Community College

4. Consider States with Low In-state Tuition Rates

Some states have a history of providing access to higher education for all citizens by keeping the tuition rate at their public universities affordable. Other states put more of their resources into state grant and scholarship programs (Cost-Saving Strategy 34) that give money directly to the students to be used for college expenses. Rather than funding institutions, this strategy allows the student to determine whether they want to go to a private or public college. The number of public colleges and universities in the state impacts the size of these state grants. In highly populated states, with few public universities, the government would rather support students at private universities than build new public colleges. This will provide a wider range of college

Key Forecast

Several state university systems will soon charge no tuition to in-state high school graduates who graduate in the top 25% of their high school class.

options. In states with a number of public institutions, the state may provide access by keeping the in-state tuition rate low. You can benefit from this lower tuition rate by becoming a resident of such states (Cost-Saving Strategy 58).

CHECKLIST

AVERAGE PRICING BY PUBLIC 4-YEAR COLLEGES AND UNIVERSITIES IN SPECIFIC STATES.

Low Priced $1,500– $2,900	Medium Priced $3,000–$4,000	High Priced $4,100–$6,000
Arizona	Alabama	Connecticut
Arkansas	Alaska	Delaware
District of Columbia	California	Maine
Florida	Colorado	Maryland
Georgia	Illinois	Massachusetts
Hawaii	Iowa	Michigan
Idaho	Kansas	Nevada
Kentucky	Minnesota	New Hampshire
Louisiana	Mississippi	New Jersey
New Mexico	Missouri	Ohio
North Carolina	Montana	Pennsylvania
Oklahoma	Nebraska	South Carolina
Tennessee	New York	Virginia
Texas	North Dakota	
West Virginia	Oregon	
	Rhode Island	
	South Dakota	
	Utah	
	Vermont	
	Washington	
	Wisconsin	
	Wyoming	

5. Study the Average Teaching Load

The single largest operating expense for a typical undergraduate college or university is faculty salaries. By asking about the average teaching load for full-time teachers, you can gain some insight into tuition prices. Schools where professors teach less than four courses per semester often have to charge higher tuition to employ more faculty members. If on average faculty members teach fewer than four courses per semester, your tuition will need to increase by 10 percent per course reduction to pay for these reduced teaching loads. Some colleges attempt to control this cost by using graduate students to teach freshman- and sophomore-level courses. This can present other problems pertaining to the quality of instruction.

6. Find a Guaranteed Tuition Rate

Put your mind at ease about tuition increases by getting a guarantee up front of what the tuition will be throughout your education. Tuition increases may be a fact of life, but there are a few ways to avoid them. Some states have begun programs that hold tuition rates for a child for up to twenty years if parents will pay into a fund in advance.

Some schools in an attempt to improve recruitment of students are offering a guarantee, usually with a shorter time frame than the state sponsored program. At these colleges, families are able to "lock-in" tuition with a guarantee that tuition will not increase for a new freshman over the course of four years of study. Another program benefits those who take more than four years to graduate by offering the fifth year "free." The student benefits in two ways: the college is motivated to help students graduate in four years, and it can be useful for students who want to take extra classes to complete work for a second degree.

All of these programs allow students and their families to plan in advance to meet educational costs.

7. Attend a Tuition-Free College

All things considered, a tuition-free education is a pretty good deal. But just like with everything else in life, "free" usually means there is a catch. The two largest classes of tuition-free programs are the United States Military Academies, which look for the best of the best and require a military service commitment after gradua- tion; and seminaries, which have benefactors or sponsors provid- ing training for new ministers or clergy (Cost-Saving Strategy 57). Some states, including California, are proposing programs that would allow any student with a specific high school record a free education at any in-state university.

THE WINNERS

INSTITUTIONS OFFERING A FREE EDUCATION

State	University
Colorado	United States Air Force Academy
Connecticut	United States Coast Guard Academy
Maryland	United States Naval Academy
New York	United States Military Academy
	United States Merchant Marines Academy

8. Don't Pay Unnecessary Student Fees

Don't let the college decide what extra services you need. Once you decide on the type of college you want to attend, narrow your list down to schools that have only those services you really need. For example, if you plan to spend only class time on campus, you don't need to support a major athletic program, entertainment center, conference center, hotel, restaurant, ice rink, community service center, hospital, chapel/church, museum, theater, swimming pool, day-care center, business center, or retreat house. Many students have their own outlets for these programs and services and don't need their college to provide them. This is especially true for students attending college in a large city.

Stat-to-Know

Some colleges charge more than $1,000 a year in fees for services you may not use.

Colleges offer a long list of student-funded facilities, programs, and services that add little to your basic education. Extras such as an art museum, performing arts center, or convention center can be very costly to operate, and that cost is passed on to students in the form of higher tuition and student fees. Every time there is an increase in a college's service budget, your fees will be increased.

If you attend college in a large city, you can find museums, theaters, and other extracurricular opportunities in the local community where they will be paid for by taxes or gate receipts rather than your tuition.

9. Commute to College

Commuting to college can save you considerable money by reducing or eliminating the cost of room, board, food service, and related expenses. If you already live near the college you wish to attend, you already have the equivalent of a large scholarship covering your room and board. The savings go beyond the cost of housing and a meal plan. You can also expect to save on expenses such as laundry, snacks, computers, entertainment, and transportation home during breaks.

In fact, the majority of today's college students are commuters, and almost every college has at least some students who live off campus. The amount of money you can save as a commuter depends on the type

Stat-to-Know

Fewer then 1 out of 5 college students live on campus.

of college you attend and the area in which the college is located. City colleges have room and board charges that are higher than at colleges in rural settings. The city schools charge almost 50 percent more on average for these services.

When selecting a college as a commuter, avoid schools that have a large percent of students living on campus. As a commuter at this type of school, you may have trouble feeling a part of the college community. You also will pay for a large complex of auxiliary services needed for housing that you will rarely use, such as dining halls, housekeeping, security, entertainment, and recreation. Colleges often "subsidize" these costs with general student fees. At these institutions even if you commute, you will pay for other students to live on campus.

It is true that commuter students do miss out on the social interaction of campus living, but you can more than make up for this by getting involved in activities at your school or by developing social contacts and relationships outside of school, such as at work, as an intern, in a church, or as a volunteer.

INSIDER'S ADVICE

WHAT TO LOOK FOR IN A COMMUTER COLLEGE

▶ Convenient transportation

▶ Adequate parking

▶ Small percent of students living on campus

▶ Opportunities for student involvement

▶ Strong adviser program

▶ Safe neighborhood

▶ Both day and evening classes

▶ Electronic mail system with faculty

▶ Open e-mail registration and student information processes

▶ Near job or home

While almost all colleges have some commuter students, many schools do not serve them well. A few colleges have designed their programs around the special needs of commuter students. Some are even exclusively commuter schools.

THE WINNERS

COLLEGES DESIGNED TO SERVE COMMUTER STUDENTS

State	University
Alabama	Troy State University-Montgomery
Arizona	Prescott College

California	Art Institute of Southern California Golden Gate University National University
Colorado	University of Colorado-Denver
Delaware	Wilmington College
District of Columbia	Southeastern University
Illinois	Northeastern Illinois University Robert Morris College Governors State University
Indiana	Indiana University-South Bend Purdue University-North Central Indiana University-Fort Wayne
Louisiana	Our Lady of Holy Cross College Southern University-New Orleans
Massachusetts	University of Massachusetts-Boston
Michigan	Cleary College Detroit College of Business Kendall College of Art & Design University of Michigan-Dearborn
Minnesota	Metropolitan State University
Nebraska	University of Nebraska-Omaha
New York	Audrey Cohen College Cooper Union College CUNY St. John's University St. Joseph's College-New York

(Continued)

COLLEGES DESIGNED TO SERVE COMMUTER STUDENTS (Continued)	
State	*University*
Ohio	Franklin University
	Lourdes College
	Union Institute
Pennsylvania	Holy Family College
Texas	University of Houston-Downtown
Washington	City University
	Heritage College

10. Don't Attend College Far from Home

Going to college a great distance from home might seem exciting, but it can add considerably to your total cost of education. Even if you elect not to come home for each break, you may pay as much to stay on campus during holidays as it would cost you to travel home. At many colleges, dorms close during breaks, so students can't stay even if they want to.

Before you decide to attend a distant college, be sure your doing so for the right reasons. A far-off college should offer an academic program— either in a specialized subject or by program reputation—that you can't find nearby. If you are thinking about

Stat-to-Know

Over 75% of college graduates return home for work.

going to college far away from home for other reasons—to cut ties with the familiar, to grow as an individual, to see new things and meet new people—you might want to consider other options. For example, joining the military or taking a year or two off to work and travel might satisfy that feeling of wanderlust. Attending a college far from home will limit your ability to establish professional contacts, find internships, or network in the area you will probably begin your career. Remember most college graduates return home to begin their careers.

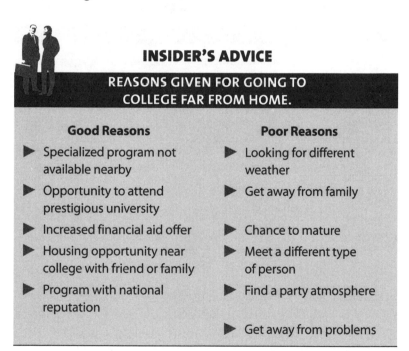

INSIDER'S ADVICE

REASONS GIVEN FOR GOING TO COLLEGE FAR FROM HOME.

Good Reasons	Poor Reasons
▶ Specialized program not available nearby	▶ Looking for different weather
▶ Opportunity to attend prestigious university	▶ Get away from family
▶ Increased financial aid offer	▶ Chance to mature
▶ Housing opportunity near college with friend or family	▶ Meet a different type of person
▶ Program with national reputation	▶ Find a party atmosphere
	▶ Get away from problems

11. Build Equity in Your College Housing

Buy rather than rent your college housing. This way you are building equity rather than putting money down a rental rat-hole. A $65,000 condo that has an extra room that you can rent to another student for say, $300 a month is actually cheaper than paying the room portion of your dorm fee or the rent on a $400-a-month apartment.

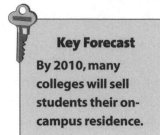

Key Forecast

By 2010, many colleges will sell students their on-campus residence.

PUTTING IT IN PERSPECTIVE

SHOULD I BUY A CONDO?

	Condominium Ownership	Living in a Dormitory	Apartment Rental
Average 5-year Cost	$41,602	$35,000	$30,000
Rent You Collect on Extra Room	$15,000		$15,000
Average Net Cost	**$26,602**	**$35,000**	**$15,000**
Less: Average Appreciation at Sale	$14,082		
True 5-year Cost	**$12,520**	**$35,000**	**$15,000**

Money you pay toward an apartment or dorm fees is gone forever. With many students today taking over six years to graduate, a good alternative is to buy a condo and then sell it after you leave school. This is an especially attractive alternative if you attend college in a large city with great resale potential.

If you select a two-bedroom unit, you can rent a room to one or two other students to help pay your mortgage. Getting the down payment is much easier today as the required amount can be as low as 5 percent. However, a dependent student will need a co-signer on the mortgage.

12. Look for Convenience Items

Adding value to your education with convenience services can save you money as long as the extra services are things you would be using anyway. Colleges across the country are competing for students by adding extra-value services. These services include everything from fitness centers, parking, day care, and health services to counseling, tutoring, and learning labs.

PROFILES

Margo is a thirty-year-old mother with two children. She plans to earn a degree in nursing at a large private university near her and husband's home. Margo figures that she saves over $400 per month by utilizing available college services. She is a regular at the fitness center and leaves her daughters, Lisa and Nina, with the staff of the campus day care center. She also participates on the club fencing team and parks at a reduced rate in the campus garage.

---

13. Don't Support Football

Football is America's most popular spectator sport, but that doesn't mean you should have to pay for it with higher tuition. At most of the top thirty Division I football programs,

Stat-to-Know

A Division I football team can eat up to 6% of your tuition dollar.

football not only covers its own operating costs but also contributes to other athletic program costs. Even when football programs at these institutions don't cover costs, the costs are usually a relatively small portion of the school's overall budget.

That is not the case at most second-tier universities. At these schools, support for major athletic programs from students, alumni, and the local community is minimal, so the costs of running the programs must be passed on to students through their tuition and fees. Football is of particular concern because its large number of scholarships, travel costs, stadium operations, size of staff, and other needs can be very expensive.

If you are planning to attend a college or university that is not perennially a top-thirty football program, you should seriously consider whether supporting football is a priority for you. At Division I NCAA schools, a football program can use up to 6 percent of your tuition dollars. This "investment" often does not pay off in terms of increased alumni networking, as is often the case at a top football school. When selecting a Division I college that is not one of the top 30 football programs, look for one that does not have Division I football.

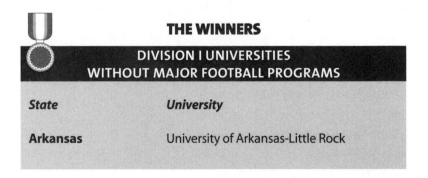

THE WINNERS

DIVISION I UNIVERSITIES WITHOUT MAJOR FOOTBALL PROGRAMS	
State	*University*
Arkansas	University of Arkansas-Little Rock

State	University
California	California State University Loyola Marymount University Pepperdine University Santa Clara University University of California-Irvine University of California-Santa Barbara University of San Francisco
District of Columbia	American University George Washington University
Georgia	Georgia State University
Illinois	Bradley University DePaul University Illinois State University Loyola University-Chicago University of Illinois-Chicago
Kansas	Wichita State University
Louisiana	University of New Orleans
Maryland	Loyola College in Maryland University of Maryland-Baltimore University of Maryland-Eastern Shore
Massachusetts	Boston University
Michigan	University of Detroit-Mercy
Missouri	Saint Louis University
Nebraska	Creighton University

(Continued)

DIVISION I UNIVERSITIES
WITHOUT MAJOR FOOTBALL PROGRAMS (Continued)

State	University
New Jersey	Fairleigh Dickerson University Seton Hall University
New York	Niagara University St. Bonaventure University St. Francis College
North Carolina	University of North Carolina-Charlotte University of North Carolina-Greensboro
Ohio	Cleveland State University Wright State University Xavier University
Oklahoma	Oral Roberts University
Oregon	University of Portland
Pennsylvania	St. Joseph's University
Rhode Island	Providence College
Texas	Lamar University Texas A&M-Corpus Christi University of Texas-Pan-American University of Texas-San Antonio
Vermont	University of Vermont
Virginia	Old Dominion University Virginia Commonwealth University
Washington	Gonzaga University
Wisconsin	Marquette University University of Wisconsin-Green Bay University of Wisconsin-Milwaukee

14. Cut Transportation Costs

Even as a commuter you can control daily transportation costs. Keep in mind that commuting students often spend an average of $50 to $200 a month for public transportation. If you decide to drive to school instead, remember that total transportation costs include parking, insurance, automobile upkeep, gas, wear and tear on the vehicle, and your driving time. That could represent a significant portion of your living budget. Review a transit map before you select a school to determine your options for getting to class. Also, take into account the quality of the school's surrounding neighborhood. This can be an important factor when accessing public transportation, especially after evening classes. Finding a car pool can be complicated with different individual schedules but can be a great cost saver.

PUTTING IT IN PERSPECTIVE

THE COST OF DRIVING TO COLLEGE AS COMMUTER			
Lease	Lease	$4,200.00	
	Maintenance	580.00	
	Insurance	1,200.00	
	Fuel	840.00	
	Annual Cost	$6,840.00	
Own	Depreciation	$4,000.00	($20,000 over 5 years)
	Maintenance	580.00	
	Insurance	1,200.00	
	Fuel	840.00	
	Interest on Loan	1,400.00	(7% on full $20,000 value)
	Annual Cost	$8,020.00	

15. Buy Your Books Early

Whether you buy your books online, in the college store, or at a private bookstore, you should get them as early as possible. The number of used books available for a course will almost always be less than the number of students enrolled. This means those who don't get them first will pay considerably more to buy new textbooks.

Some experts predict that the price of printed books will moderate with the advent of electronic publishing and online books. Yet the lucrative market of textbooks may be an exception to that good news. It's true that the "electronic book universe" may benefit students by providing more up-to-date and better-focused material that is more closely tied to course objectives. But electronic books also will make used books obsolete, requiring students to always buy new books.

16. Join a Cooperative

Although the number of student cooperatives has actually declined in the past ten years, they still can be found on many campuses. Student cooperatives can save you money, as they pass on their savings from group purchases and from coop members providing low- or no-cost staffing to the store.

Cooperatives take a number of different forms. There are book cooperatives, where you can often purchase books, supplies, and soft goods at below normal retail rates. Housing cooperatives allow you to work (in housekeeping, food service, security, etc.) in exchange for reduced living costs. Some of these housing coops also develop a strong sense of family among residents, adding an additional benefit. Check admissions offices or student newspapers for more information about coops.

PROFILES

Connie was an eighteen-year-old freshman at a college 500 miles from home. She knew no one. Her accounting major had her taking classes off the main campus at a downtown site. When Connie arrived on campus, she was not happy to find all of the regular dorms full. She was sent to a housing coop to find a room. Once she moved in she found the coop to be a perfect fit. She saved money by taking on kitchen/shopping duty, and felt like she belonged in a new "family" away from home. Two of her housemates were also attending class downtown and were happy to show her the ropes.

17. Buying Technology Through the College

Technology has quickly become an essential tool—and one more cost—for college students. Some schools require that all incoming students purchase computers, or they provide the equipment to all students and add the cost to student fees. At other colleges they provide computers to students in particular programs with the understanding that they must return them at the end of the term.

Most colleges also offer students the opportunity to purchase computers at a substantial discount, ranging from 20 to 30 percent off list price. If you are interested in purchasing, be sure to talk to other students about the quality of service and reliability of the equipment before taking advantage of these buying opportunities. While prices offered by some colleges may not seem to be that much lower than retail, their support systems may make it a worthwhile choice.

CHAPTER 4

Buy Fewer Terms of Study

There is definitely truth in the statement *Time is Money* when it comes to college planning. The strategies in this section will help you find ways to cut your time to degree and the number of terms (semesters/quarters) of college that you need to pay for. Today's student takes nearly six years on average to complete an undergraduate degree. This is 1.5 years longer than the average of twenty years ago. Not only does this additional time to graduation increase out-of-pocket costs, but often little or no financial aid is available for those extra years. More significantly, that extra time in school delays your income earning years. The strategies and tips in this section will help you find ways to cut the time it takes you to finish your degree and thus reduce the resulting costs.

18. Consider Earning a Dual Degree

Combining your bachelor's program with a graduate or professional degree can save you considerable time and money because some of the coursework will count toward both degrees. About one-third of all colleges and universities offer combined degrees. Usually, the degrees are earned from one university, but there are some programs that allow you to earn the degrees from two partnering institutions.

43

Completing a dual-degree program requires considerable planning and works best when you are sure of your career goals. When you begin a dual-degree program, you are making a major commitment to two sets of requirements. These programs are often particularly attractive to transfer students, who may have a clearer idea of their long-term educational goals.

CHECKLIST

POPULAR DUAL-DEGREE PROGRAMS

▶ Bachelor of Arts and Masters of Business Administration

▶ Bachelor of Arts and Masters of Science in a Technology Field

▶ Bachelor of Arts and Masters of Library and Information Sciences

▶ Bachelor of Arts and Juris Doctor

▶ Bachelor of Architecture and Masters of Business Administration

▶ Bachelor of Architecture and Bachelor of Engineering

▶ Bachelor of Science and Masters of Education

▶ Bachelor of Science and Doctor of Medicine

▶ Bachelor of Arts and Bachelor of Science

Dual-degree programs save valuable time and provide tuition savings. When undergraduate coursework counts toward graduate degrees, the cost savings can be considerable when students are charged less costly undergraduate tuition rates for the graduate credit.

PROFILES

Ellie has always wanted to be a pediatrician. The only part she found unattractive was the number of years required to get through school. She searched for and found a program that admitted her to a dual degree in chemistry and medicine. It allowed her to begin med. school in her fourth year of college.

19. Earn a Certificate in a Career Field

You don't have to earn a degree to become an expert in a field. In today's rapidly changing world, even college graduates will need to update their skills throughout their working lives. No one can afford to sit back and coast through a career. To meet this need for constant updating, colleges have developed thousands of certificate programs, which are designed to teach specialized skills, in a highly focused area, over a short time period.

Although aimed at people already in the work world, these certificate programs also are open to those without college degrees and they can be an excellent way to acquire marketable skills in a relatively short time. Completing a certificate program before enrolling in a degree program also is a good way to sample an area of study to see if you like it. You can always earn the related degree later. And if the certificate helps you land a job related to the field of study, your employer may pay your tuition if you decide to pursue the degree on a part-time basis. You are then earning and learning at the same time.

You can be certain that a certificate of interest to you is being offered by a credible college. There are many for-profit institutions that offer these types of certificates but the credit they award may not transfer to a college at a later date. Things to look for when selecting a certificate program include: credits that will transfer to a degree program; courses taught by regular college faculty; technology that is up-to-date; students required to demonstrate proficiency; open to undergraduate students; and specially priced.

Certificate programs go by a variety of names, so you may need to do some research to find programs that fit your need.

CHECKLIST

COMMON TYPES OF PRE-DEGREE CERTIFICATE PROGRAMS

▶ Corporate Communication

▶ Leadership

▶ Sports/Entertainment

▶ Management

▶ Entrepreneurship

▶ Computer Design and Applications

▶ AutoCAD

▶ E-Commerce

▶ Fund Raising Management

▶ Web Design

▶ Web Commerce

▶ Web Developer

▶ Visual C++

▶ Java Developer

▶ Windows Software Development

▶ LAN

▶ Telecommunications

▶ CIS

▶ Gerontology Studies and Substance Abuse

▶ Cookery Certificate and Baking and Pastry Certificate

▶ Java Programming

▶ Networks: Object-Oriented

▶ Software Development

▶ Environmental Studies

▶ Business Administration

▶ Finance

▶ Information Systems

COMMON TYPES OF PRE-DEGREE
CERTIFICATE PROGRAMS (Continued)

- ► Marketing
- ► Operations Management
- ► Organizational & Business
- ► Communication
- ► Public Relations
- ► Writing for Media
- ► Database Applications
- ► Creative Writing
- ► Graphic Design
- ► Playwriting
- ► Studio Art
- ► International Studies
- ► French Language
- ► German Language
- ► Italian Language
- ► Spanish Language
- ► Mathematics
- ► Statistics
- ► Microsoft Certified
- ► Systems Engineer
- ► Administrative
- ► Techniques
- ► Business
- ► Pre-health Professions
- ► Writing
- ► Hospitality Management
- ► Conflict Resolution

(Continued)

COMMON TYPES OF PRE-DEGREE CERTIFICATE PROGRAMS (Continued)

▶ Athletic Training

▶ Information Systems

▶ Network Administration

▶ Banking and Financial Services

▶ Building/Property Management

▶ Fire Protection

▶ Health Assistance

▶ Child Care

▶ Computer Maintenance

▶ Construction Trades

▶ Cosmetology

▶ Culinary Arts

▶ Dental Assisting

▶ Electrical Equipment

▶ Heating, Air Conditioning, and Refrigeration

▶ Horticultural Studies

▶ Industrial Electronics

▶ Landscaping

▶ Library Assistance

▶ Mechanical Drafting

▶ Medical Administrative

▶ Paralegal

▶ Parks, Recreation, and Leisure Studies

▶ Practical Nurse (LPN)

▶ Quality Control

▶ Real Estate

▶ Travel Services

20. Design a Transfer Plan

The majority of students will transfer before earning their degree. You can't always plan ahead for a later transfer, but if you are attending a community college you know you will be changing schools. If you are using a community college as the first step to a degree, it's essential that you develop a transfer plan from the beginning. Starting at a community college will only save you money if you adequately plan and prepare. Your course selection at the community college is crucial. If you spend time at a community college and later can't transfer the credits, you have defeated your own cost-saving strategy and instead wasted time and money. While each individual case is different, having a detailed transfer plan can make the difference between a successful college strategy and one that lacks benefit.

The first step in building a transfer plan is to determine which senior institutions (the college you plan to earn your bachelor's degree from) you might eventually attend. Once you have a school in mind, review the articulation agreements between your community college and those schools. Articulation agreements describe which courses will transfer and what degree requirements those courses fulfill at the senior college.

If you don't know exactly which school you want to transfer to, look for community colleges that have a large number of articulation agreements with other schools. Many states have a standard, statewide articulation program between its community colleges and state universities in which the universities agree to fit a standard community college curriculum into their own so students don't lose any academic credits when transferring in.

Don't wait until you change schools to investigate transfer issues. If possible, try to learn which course credits will and will not transfer to your chosen senior college. You should also ensure that all of the work you do at the community college transfers to the major you are considering at the senior institution (Cost-Saving Strategy 1). Try to find out how many students in your intended major have transferred from community colleges.

It's also important to review the admissions requirements and the number of spots available each year to transfer students. Most colleges use a different set of criteria to evaluate transfer student applications than they do for new freshman applicants. The most important difference is that high school GPA, high school rank in class, and standardized test scores are less important for transfer student applicants. Transfer students are evaluated heavily on college GPA. Consider transferring into a senior institution in the winter or spring, rather than the traditional fall start. Many colleges have more seats available for transfer students in the spring or winter terms.

INSIDER'S ADVICE

COURSES THAT USUALLY TRANSFER

▶ Principles of Financial Accounting

▶ Principles of Managerial Accounting

▶ Introduction to Social and Cultural Anthropology

▶ Introduction to Physical Anthropology

▶ Fundamentals of Two-Dimensional Art

▶ Fundamentals of Three-Dimensional Art

▶ Art History

▶ Introduction to Life Science

▶ College Biology

▶ Human Anatomy and Physiology

▶ Business Law

COURSES THAT USUALLY TRANSFER (Continued)

▶ Principles of Finance

▶ College Chemistry

▶ Organic Chemistry

▶ Managing Information Systems

▶ Computer Science

▶ Numerical Methods

▶ Programming

▶ Earth Science

▶ Economics

▶ Composition I

▶ Composition II

▶ Introduction to Literature

▶ French I

▶ French II

▶ German I

▶ German II

▶ Hebrew I

▶ Hebrew II

▶ United States History to 1877

▶ United States History from 1877

▶ Western Civilization to 1560

▶ Western Civilization from 1650

▶ Introduction to Art

▶ Introduction to Music

▶ Philosophy

▶ Japanese I

▶ Japanese II

(Continued)

COURSES THAT USUALLY TRANSFER (Continued)

▶ Korean I

▶ Korean II

▶ Intermediate Algebra

▶ Trigonometry

▶ Statistics

▶ Calculus I

▶ Calculus II

▶ Principles of Management

▶ Principles of Marketing

▶ College Physics

▶ American Government

▶ Political Science

▶ Introduction to Psychology

▶ Introduction to Sociology

▶ Spanish I

▶ Spanish II

PROFILES

Ramon and his brother John, nineteen and twenty-one respectively, went to the local community college together. Ramon took a general education based transfer program. John enrolled in a horticulture management program. After two years of full-time study, the brothers transferred together to a large private university and enrolled in a business administration program. All of Ramon's earned credits transferred, while only 27 of John's 64 earned credits transferred in.

21. Select the Right College for You

If you don't select the right type of college in the first place and end up transferring, you will increase your time to graduation and the total cost of earning your degree. First select the right type of college and then zero in on the right school.

Key Forecast

Over 75% of today's college freshman will transfer before earning a bachelor's degree

Students often select a college based upon peer pressure and other dated methods of college selection. Every college and every student is unique. A good college choice will be the best match possible between what the college uniquely has to offer and your special needs. Don't be impressed by the dozens of students from your high school enrolling at some college a thousand miles from home because it's a "popular choice."

Every prospective college student should be able to list at least three reasons that one college choice is better than all other alternatives. Those three reasons should stand the test of family and advisor scrutiny.

INSIDER'S ADVICE

WHAT TO CONSIDER
WHEN SELECTING A COLLEGE

Career Development—The number one reason most students attend college is career or job preparation. If this is the case for you, be sure all of your potential college choices focus on career, or applied education. Applied education should include: internships and externships, practitioner-based instruction, and job placement that gets results.

(Continued)

WHAT TO CONSIDER WHEN
SELECTING A COLLEGE (Continued)

Major—Be sure your college choice is strong in your chosen field of study.

Reputation—The college's reputation in the business community will become part of your reputation after graduation.

Technology—Technology should be found in every course. A college must be centered on technology rather than on information. Learning today should include systems of data capture, analysis, and applications to problem solving.

Cost—Can you afford the cost of tuition after aid awards?

Convenience —A good choice will fit your life. The best college for you will give you flexible study and course options that work for you.

22. Pick the Appropriate Field of Study

You can enter most career fields from a number of different college majors. Often, students will select a major that is the traditional approach to entry to a career field, without considering related fields of study that might be better choices for them. By looking at related subject areas, students may discover a major that fits their abilities and interests better than the traditional entry major for their chosen career field.

For example, students who have an initial interest in computer science may find the coursework in computer programming easier or more interesting. They might also consider programs in information systems, computer studies, computer technology, computer networking, or telecommunications. While related majors may not be any easier, they may be a better match with your learning style (Cost-Saving Strategy 74) and time commitment. If you are planning to earn a graduate degree in computer science, you need to ask yourself if an information systems major combining computers and business is a better choice than computer science as an undergraduate major. The right course of study will help you make progress toward a degree and give you a greater chance of accomplishing your other end goals.

PUTTING IT IN PERSPECTIVE

RELATED DEGREE SUBJECT AREAS

Traditional Major	Other Related Majors	
▶ Public Accounting	▶ Management Accounting	▶ Business Administration
▶ Computer Science	▶ Information Systems	▶ Computer Technology
▶ Telecommunications	▶ Network Management	▶ Network Technology
▶ Aeronautical Engineering	▶ Aerospace Engineering Technology	▶ Aerospace Technology
▶ Architecture	▶ Architecture Technology	▶ Architectural Drafting
▶ Nursing	▶ Medical Assisting	▶ Nurse's Aide
▶ Chemical Engineering	▶ Chemistry	▶ Physical Science
▶ Biology	▶ General Science	▶ Laboratory Technology

(Continued)

RELATED DEGREE SUBJECT AREAS (Continued)

Traditional Major	Other Related Majors	
▶ Biomedical Engineering	▶ Biomedical Engineering Technology	▶ Biomedical Equipment Technology
▶ Construction Engineering	▶ Building Construction Technology	▶ Computer Aided Drafting (C.A.D.)
▶ Environmental Engineering	▶ Environmental Management	▶ Environmental Studies
▶ Industrial Engineering	▶ Industrial Technology	▶ Industrial Supervision
▶ Material Science	▶ Material Management	▶ Material Technology
▶ Web Design	▶ Web Commerce	▶ Web Retailing
▶ Physical Therapy	▶ Physical Therapy Assistant	▶ Medical Aide
▶ Occupational Therapy	▶ Occupational Therapy Assistant	▶ Occupational Aide
▶ Medicine	▶ Physician's Assistant	▶ Medical Assistant
▶ Dentistry	▶ Dental Hygiene	▶ Dental Assistant
▶ Hospitality Management	▶ Restaurant Management	▶ Culinary Studies
▶ Sports Medicine	▶ Athletic Podiatry	▶ Athletic Training

(Continued)

RELATED DEGREE SUBJECT AREAS (Continued)		
Traditional Major	**Other Related Majors**	
▶ Wireless System Design	▶ Wireless Programming	▶ Wireless System Management
▶ Psychology	▶ Educational Counseling	▶ Geriatric Counseling
▶ Pharmacology Technology	▶ Pharmacy	▶ Pharmaceutical Technician

Selecting a major related to your initial choice allows you to find a better match with your aptitude, learning style, time commitment, career plans, and personality. It should also increase your chances of finishing your degree and graduating on time.

PROFILES

Manny was always good in math and felt accounting would be a good major choice even though he knew that he did not want to work in a public accounting settings. Once enrolled in college he found that managerial accounting was a better choice for him. It used more math and better prepared him to work in his chosen career field.

---

23. Select a Major Before You Start

Determine what your major will be before you select a college, since schools have different academic strengths and program emphases. If you have no idea what your major will be, it will be difficult to make a good college choice. You will not know what it is that you are looking for in a school.

Determining your major is a turning point in your life. It will influence your future career options and lifestyle alternatives. It's a manageable process if you view the selection of a major as a way of prioritizing your options. It might be easier to think in terms of a first and second choice, or even of having several alternatives, in case you decide your initial choice isn't a good fit. Once you know your alternatives, select a school that offers at least your top two choices of fields of study.

Many students change majors one, two, or more times. A change in major almost always means additional time to graduation, but the real danger is that it may require a change in college. If that happens, the cost of your degree goes up dramatically because transferring schools usually adds extra semesters. Remember, extra terms of study add to your costs in two ways: (1) additional out-of-pocket expenses for tuition and (2) lost wages you would have earned if you weren't still in school. Together these costs can easily amount to $50,000 or more for an extra year of college.

You can explore potential majors through reading, meeting with professionals in various career areas, and by taking assessment inventories. These assessment tools are often available at high schools or at your local community college. Taking exploratory coursework at a community college can also be used to find the best major fit.

PUTTING IT IN PERSPECTIVE

	TYPICAL TRANSFER STUDENT'S BACHELOR'S DEGREE CALENDAR					
Sum Fall Spr	Sum Fall Spr	Sum Fall Spr	Sum Fall Spr	Sum Fall Spr	Sum Fall Spr	
Student 1st Year	Student 2nd Year	Student 3rd Year	Student 4th Year	Student 5th Year	Student 6th Year	

	ON-TIME BACHELOR'S DEGREE CALENDAR					
Sum Fall Spr	Sum Fall Spr	Sum Fall Spr	Sum Fall Spr	Sum Fall Spr	Sum Fall Spr	
Student 1st Year	Student 2nd Year	Student 3rd Year	Student 4th Year	WORKING IN YOUR FIELD 5th Year	6th Year	

PROFILES

John was always good at science and math, so he enrolled in a science honors program at a small private university. In his sophomore year, he had an internship at a local engineering firm and fell in love with the applied nature of engineering. But when he decided to change his major to engineering, he discovered his university didn't have an engineering program. Transferring to another school meant three additional semesters to graduation. This cost him both money and income opportunity, since he was still in school when he should have been working full-time.

24. Establish Career Goals Early

A major is a field of study while a career is a working life. They are two very different things. Not every freshman knows exactly what he or she is going to do after graduation. But making that decision as soon as possible is one of the best ways to cut your overall college costs. If you already have a chosen career in mind, you'll be able to focus on career development and speed your way to graduation, whether you're working toward an associate's or bachelor's degree.

If you haven't fully decided on your career path or if you foresee breaks in your education, it can be very beneficial to complete coursework in marketable, skill related subjects early in your education. These marketable skills are usually in applied fields, such as web design, network management, information systems, accounting, medical assisting, programming, health care technology, etc. You can use these skills to land a job while still enrolled in school. Employers like to hire continuing students who have these types of specific skills that they can use on the job, and the on-the-job experience in your chosen fields will be very helpful to you after graduation.

To acquire marketable skills early, your curriculum plan should allow you to take major coursework from the first term of your enrollment. Avoid colleges that tell you that you can't take courses in your major until your junior year. Your coursework should equip you with valuable job skills early on in the program and emphasize career development throughout your course of study. Colleges that offer both associate's and bachelor's degrees often do this well. Their students earn an associate's degree on the way to earning their bachelor's degree. Because the associate's degree is often seen as a stand-alone degree, students develop marketable skills early in their studies making them more employable while still in college.

THE WINNERS

COLLEGES THAT OFFER BOTH ASSOCIATE'S AND BACHELOR'S DEGREES

State	University
Arkansas	University of the Ozarks
Connecticut	University of Connecticut
Florida	Florida State University
Georgia	University of Georgia
Hawaii	Brigham Young University – Hawaii Campus
Illinois	Robert Morris College
Indiana	Indiana University
Louisiana	Tulane University
Massachusetts	University of Massachusetts-Amherst
Maine	University of Maine-Augusta
Michigan	Adrian College
Minnesota	University of Minnesota
Montana	Western Montana College of the University of Montana
Nebraska	University of Nebraska
New Hampshire	University of New Hampshire
New Mexico	New Mexico State University
New York	State University of New York
North Carolina	North Carolina State University-Raleigh
Ohio	Ohio University
Pennsylvania	Pennsylvania State-University Park
Utah	Utah State University
Vermont	Champlain College
Virginia	Virginia Polytechnic Institute and State University
West Virginia	West Virginia University

The majority of students are unable to go straight through college without taking a break for one reason or another. If you have to leave school for a term, a year, or several years, it helps to be prepared for the world of work with marketable skills.

PROFILES

When she started college, Sandra expected to go straight through and earn her bachelor's degree in four years. But midway into her junior year, her parents divorced, affecting Sandra's financial resources for school. She had to leave school that year to earn enough money to finish her degree, but she had no marketable skills at that point. In her first two and half years of college, she had taken only general coursework rather than getting into her major field of study, which was accounting. It wasn't Sandra's fault: her college required students to achieve junior status before being accepted into their major department of study. Without marketable skills, she had to settle for low-paying work as a waitress, which meant it took her even longer to save for her return to school.

Jesus also had to leave school after two years when his father died. But since he had already earned an associate's degree in computer networking, Jesus was able to choose from many high-paying job offers, including one that provided tuition reimbursement. Now Jesus works during the day and goes to school at night. It will take him a little longer than he expected to earn his degree, but his employer is paying his tuition, he is earning a good income, and he is gaining valuable work experience while still in college.

25. Time to Graduation

The time it takes to earn your degree is one of the most important components in controlling your college costs. Although some students still graduate in four years or less, it is far more likely they will need over six years to finish a degree. Failure to graduate on plan can be costly. Students who don't graduate in four years spend, on average, 30 percent more for tuition than those who complete school in four years or less. Students are too often caught off-guard by this extra time to graduation. For these students, it usually isn't part of their original financial plan to pay for six or seven years of college.

Some colleges have a better record than others in graduating their students in four years or less. Since buying fewer semesters or quarters of study is the best way to save on college costs, look for a college that has a record of helping its students graduate in a timely fashion. You should ask college admission counselors what the average graduation time is in your major area of study. You can also find this information in a number of college guidebooks that profile American colleges and universities.

THE WINNERS

COLLEGES WITH SPECIAL PROGRAMS TO INSURE GRADUATION IN 4 YEARS

State	University
California	California Institute of Technology
	Harvey Mudd College
	Loyola Marymount University

(Continued)

COLLEGES WITH SPECIAL PROGRAMS TO INSURE GRADUATION IN 4 YEARS (Continued)

State	University
California (continued)	Pepperdine University
	St. Mary's College of California
	Santa Clara University
	Stanford University
Colorado	Colorado College
	University of Denver
Connecticut	Connecticut College
	Fairfield University
	St. Joseph College
	Trinity College
	United States Coast Guard Academy
	Yale University
Delaware	University of Delaware
District of Columbia	American University
	Catholic University of America
	George Washington University
	Georgetown University
Florida	Eckerd College
	Ringling School of Art & Design
Georgia	Oglethorpe University
Illinois	Augustana College
	Illinois Wesleyan University
	Knox College
	Lake Forest College
	Millikan University
	Northwestern University
	Robert Morris College
	University of Chicago

COLLEGES WITH SPECIAL PROGRAMS TO INSURE GRADUATION IN 4 YEARS (Continued)

State	*University*
Indiana	DePauw University
	Earlham College
	Hanover College
	Rose-Hulman Institute of Technology
	St. Mary's College
	University of Notre Dame
	Wabash College
Iowa	Coe College
	Cornell College
	Drake University
	Grinnell College
Kentucky	Centre College
	Transylvania University
Maine	Bates College
	Bowdoin College
	Colby College
Maryland	College of Notre Dame of Maryland
	Johns Hopkins University
	St. John's College
	St. Mary's College of Maryland
	United States Naval Academy
	Washington College
Massachusetts	Amherst College
	Bentley College
	Boston College
	Boston University
	Brandeis University
	Clark University

(Continued)

State	University
COLLEGES WITH SPECIAL PROGRAMS TO INSURE GRADUATION IN 4 YEARS (Continued)	
Massachusetts (continued)	College of the Holy Cross
	Massachusetts Institute of Technology
	Mount Holyoke College
	Smith College
	Springfield College
	Tufts University
	Wellesley College
	Wheaton College
	Williams College
Michigan	Albion College
	Hillsdale College
	Kalamazoo College
	University of Michigan
Minnesota	Carleton College
	College of St. Benedict
	Macalester College
	St. John's University/ College of St. Benedict
	St. Olaf College
Mississippi	Millsaps College
Missouri	Washington University
	William Jewell College
Nebraska	Creighton University
New Hampshire	Dartmouth College
	St. Anselm College
New Jersey	Drew University
	Rutgers University
	College of New Jersey

COLLEGES WITH SPECIAL PROGRAMS TO INSURE GRADUATION IN 4 YEARS (Continued)

State	University
New York	SUNY-Binghamton
	Canisius College
	Colgate University
	Columbia University
	Cooper Union College
	Cornell University
	Fordham University
	Ithaca College
	Marist College
	Nazareth College of Rochester
	New York University
	St. Bonaventure University
	St. John Fisher College
	St. Lawrence University
	Siena College
	Skidmore College
	St. Joseph's College-New York
	SUNY
	Syracuse University
	Union College
	United States Military Academy
	University of Rochester
	Vassar College
	Webb Institute
North Carolina	Davidson College
	Duke University
	Salem College
	University of North Carolina

(Continued)

COLLEGES WITH SPECIAL PROGRAMS TO INSURE GRADUATION IN 4 YEARS (Continued)

State	University
Ohio	College of Wooster
	Denison University
	John Carroll University
	Kenyon College
	Miami University-Oxford
	Oberlin College
	Ohio Wesleyan University
	University of Dayton
	Xavier University
Oregon	Lewis & Clark College
	University of Portland
	Willamette University
Pennsylvania	Bryn Mawr College
	Bucknell University
	Carnegie Mellon University
	Holy Family College
	Immaculata College
	Lafayette College
	LaSalle University
	Lehigh University
	Pennsylvania State-University Park
	St. Francis College
	St. Joseph's University
	Swarthmore College
	University of Scranton
	Villanova University
Rhode Island	Brown University
	Johnson & Wales University

COLLEGES WITH SPECIAL PROGRAMS TO INSURE GRADUATION IN 4 YEARS (Continued)

State	University
Rhode Island	Providence College
South Carolina	The Citadel
	Erskine College
	Furman University
Tennessee	Rhodes College
	University of the South
	Vanderbilt University
Texas	Rice University
	Southern Methodist University
	Trinity University
	University of Dallas
Vermont	Middlebury College
	St. Michael's College
	University of Vermont
Virginia	College of William & Mary
	James Madison University
	Randolph Macon College
	Sweet Briar College
	University of Richmond
	University of Virginia
Washington	Gonzaga University
	University of Puget Sound
Wisconsin	Alverno College
	Beloit College
	Lawrence University
	St. Norbert College
	University of Wisconsin

26. Take Advanced Placement Courses

Over the past decade, an increasing number of students have earned college credits while still in high school through the Advanced Placement (AP) program. This is a way of getting a head start on college. High school students take AP courses in a wide variety of subject areas, often taking more than one course. In some high schools, half of the students will graduate with two or more AP courses completed. Whether or not these courses are accepted by individual colleges or academic departments depends on several factors, including your scores on the AP examination. If accepted, these course credits can apply toward your major or toward general education requirements.

For many reasons, AP courses aren't always transferred into college credit. You may not score well enough to earn credit, the courses may not fit your curriculum, or you may feel the need to retake the class at the college level. As colleges look for new ways to increase revenue, there is concern that some will make it more difficult for students to earn AP credit, since they lose tuition for each AP credit they accept.

Even if a college doesn't accept all of your AP credits, taking AP courses can be beneficial. The classes give you the opportunity to test college-level coursework and subject areas, and they look impressive on transcripts supporting college applications. AP grades also can boost your GPA by offering more quality points than non-AP high school courses. For example, an "A" grade in an AP class may be worth 5 GPA points at your high school, compared to a non-AP "A" grade which is worth only 4 points.

PROFILES

Betty and Mary both had similar grades and extracurricular activities in high school and were planning to attend college together at one of the top midwestern state universities. Betty took two Advance Placement courses in her junior year and two more as a senior. Mary didn't believe in starting college work early and took none.

Even though only one of her AP courses was accepted for credit, Betty's AP courses helped her win admission to the university. Her application was highlighted by having done so well in all four AP courses. Mary did not get accepted.

27. Attend School Year-Round

One way to finish college in less time is to attend school year-round, during the summer or during other typical vacation periods. By looking for a college that offers year-round classes and by planning course sequences in advance, you can graduate in as few as three years, instead of the national average of over five years. While some colleges offer limited course selections during summer or winter break, others let you take a full semester of credit during the summer term. Some colleges now promise students that they will not get "closed out" of required courses if they take them in a preplanned sequence. All of this can lead to big savings, which if invested could pay huge dividends.

PUTTING IT IN PERSPECTIVE

COMPARISON OF STUDENTS' COLLEGE CALENDARS

ACCELERATED YEAR ROUND BACHELOR'S DEGREE CALENDAR

Sum	Fall	Spr	Sum	Fall	Spr	Sum	Fall	Spr	Sum

1st year of college	2nd year of college	3rd year of college

TRADITIONAL BACHELOR'S DEGREE CALENDAR

Sum	Fall	Spr	Sum	Fall	Spr	Sum	Fall	Spr	Sum	Fall	Spr	Sum	Fall	Spr	Sum	Fall	Spr

1st Year of college	2nd Year of college	3rd Year of college	4th Year of college	5th Year of college	6th Year of college

INSIDER'S ADVICE

HOW TO ACCELERATE YOUR TIME TO DEGREE.

DO	DON'T
▶ Look for colleges that promote accelerated time to graduation	▶ Drop courses
▶ Plan your full program before starting college	▶ Schedule less than a full load in a term
▶ Review past summer course lists to insure the offerings will be there when you need them	▶ Take electives during the first year of college
▶ Get an Advisor to sign off on your accelerated plan	▶ Major in an area that has few students at the college
▶ Manage prerequisites carefully	▶ Take courses out of the required sequence

28. Academic Calendars

Design your own calendar. Today's college students demand more flexibility in scheduling and many colleges are responding by redesigning their academic calendars. Throughout much of the history of higher education, school calendars have been based on an agrarian lifestyle. Students would attend school from late fall to late spring, so they would be available in summer and early fall to work on the family farm. Although this calendar is of little practical value today, it is still the calendar of most colleges and universities.

But some colleges have developed new academic calendars, on both the semester and quarter basis, that better suit today's students who juggle college with work, family, and other commitments. Colleges

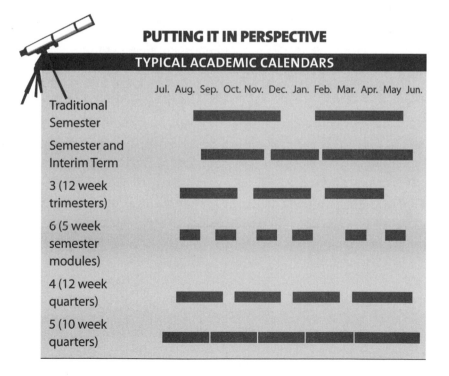

PUTTING IT IN PERSPECTIVE

TYPICAL ACADEMIC CALENDARS

	Jul.	Aug.	Sep.	Oct.	Nov.	Dec.	Jan.	Feb.	Mar.	Apr.	May	Jun.
Traditional Semester												
Semester and Interim Term												
3 (12 week trimesters)												
6 (5 week semester modules)												
4 (12 week quarters)												
5 (10 week quarters)												

that have large numbers of older adult students tend to be leaders in this type of programming. These more flexible calendars allow you to pick and choose when you want to attend classes and often offer classes on a year-round schedule.

Not only do these newer academic calendars allow flexibility, they also offer different learning options for busy students. For example, some schedules allow students to take one class at a time during intensive, short terms or modules lasting five to seven weeks. For a student juggling school with work and other commitments, studying one subject at a time allows them to remain more focused. In order to give the program a more traditional feel, two or three of these modules can be grouped into a semester. Making this nontraditional calendar look more traditional helps maintain the availability of financial aid, which is usually based on a traditional calendar. A traditional looking calendar is also easy for employers to understand when determining an employee's eligibility for tuition reimbursement.

Look for academic calendars that don't have a lot of breaks and that have combined the breaks into one extended period. By not stopping your education for repeated breaks you will finish sooner and get into the professional work world. You will be earning money while your classmates are still students. A secondary benefit of these "nontraditional" calendars is that, to take full advantage of them, you need to have a well thought out, structured plan: one that has no wasted coursework and that fills every quarter to the maximum you can handle.

29. Course Load

Students take a number of different course loads. On a typical semester calendar full-time students may take anywhere from 12 to 18 credit hours each semester. A student on a quarter schedule would take 12 to 20 quarter hours to be a full-time student. At most colleges a student needs an average of 120 semester hours to graduate. So a student needs to take 15 semester hours per semester on average to graduate in four years without attending summers. This, however, assumes that you take only classes that meet graduation requirements, that you get all courses in the sequence of prerequisites at the time you need them, and that you meet the required grade in each major course. That is a lot to have fall in place.

It is a good idea to build some wiggle room into your planning, so that a single setback does not knock you off your graduation track. Many student get into trouble by dropping courses whenever they don't like a faculty member's style or course outline. Others fall off track when they change majors and have to meet a different set of requirements.

INSIDER'S ADVICE

· SCHEDULING FOR SUCCESS

▶ Don't drop classes

▶ Take heavier course loads in your first two years

▶ Bring in AP course credit

▶ Take coursework at a community college in the summer before enrolling in college

▶ Have a set course plan approved in writing before starting

▶ Know your major before scheduling your first courses

▶ Attend summer school each year

CHAPTER 5

Scholarships, Grants, and Other Financial Aid

The strategies in this section will help you find common and creative ways to increase the financial assistance you receive. Financial aid comes from a number of sources—the college you attend, outside agencies, and government sources. This section focuses on grants, scholarships, loans, and the financial aid planning strategies available to students and parents.

30. Look for Tuition Discounts

Nearly everyone can get tuition discounts, which are commonly called institutional scholarships or grants. Colleges, especially private ones, have dramatically increased the amount of tuition discounts that they give their students. They give these discounts for the same reason that any business would: they want to increase business. In this case, that means increasing the number of students attending their college or

> **Stat-to-Know**
>
> The average tuition discount at private colleges and universities is 33%.

university. Sometimes the schools want to increase a certain "type" of student, such as minorities, top scholars, or women. On average, private colleges discount tuition by about one-third, a much larger percentage than public colleges or universities would offer. But this is only because the average private college tuition is so much higher than that at public institutions.

College tuition discounts vary greatly from school to school. However, private schools that have tougher admissions standards will discount less than those that are easier to get into. The rules are somewhat different for the very top private, prestigious (Cost-Saving Strategy 86) colleges. These schools have larger scholarship funds and will offer any discount needed to get the students that they want. For our purposes here, private colleges fall into four groups: those that accept less than 10 percent of applications (very difficult to gain admission); those that accept less than 50 percent of those that apply (difficult); those that accept about 75 percent of those applying (less difficult); and, those that accept nearly everyone that applies (very easy). When asked, college admission staffs will tell you the rate of acceptance for each incoming class at their college. You can then use the table below to get a general idea of aid-awarding practices at the college.

31. Negotiate Your Aid Package

If you have twenty students in a college course, they may be paying twenty different net tuition rates (after financial aid). This happens because colleges give institutional aid to those students they want the most. You can play this game to your advantage by leveraging one school's award offer against that of another college. When your chosen colleges fall in the same class or grouping (Cost-Saving Strategy 34), you can often let the admissions staff at one

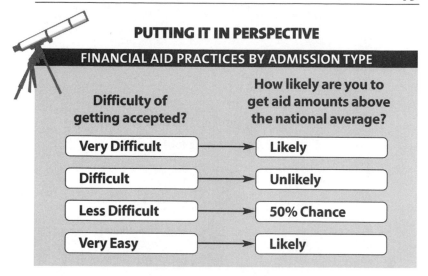

PUTTING IT IN PERSPECTIVE

FINANCIAL AID PRACTICES BY ADMISSION TYPE

Difficulty of getting accepted?	How likely are you to get aid amounts above the national average?
Very Difficult	Likely
Difficult	Unlikely
Less Difficult	50% Chance
Very Easy	Likely

college know of awards you have been offered by another college and start a bidding war—you can't beat that! Each year, a greater share of institutional aid goes to students based on their ability or special talent (merit based awards). In some cases, this reduces the amount of money awarded on a financial-need basis. As a general rule, however, colleges award aid based on a combination of financial need and ability.

Financial aid can be difficult to estimate when you consider the balance of awarding criteria used in the decision from ability and need, to your overall desirability to a college. The chart presented below gives you a basic indication of how these variables combine to affect your chances of receiving aid.

If you plan to use this strategy to set one college against another in a bidding war, you must be careful not to sacrifice an offer you already have when playing one college's aid proposal against another. Are you a good candidate for negotiating aid between colleges? This can be hard to determine. A prospective student who looks attractive to

PUTTING IT IN PERSPECTIVE

PROBABILITY OF RECEIVING ABOVE AVERAGE FINANCIAL AID AMOUNTS

Income (AGI)	$5,000	$15,000	$25,000	$35,000	$45,000	$55,000	$65,000	$75,000	$85,000	Income (AGI)
A 36										1600
32		HIGH								1550 S
A 28										1350
A 24										1150
C 20				AVERAGE						950 A
T™ 16										750 T™
12										550
8							LOW			350
4										150
0										0

This graph above represents a student's probability of receiving significant financial aid from grants and scholarships. To determine where you stand, find the point at which your ACT or SAT score and your familys adjusted gross income (AGI) meet. The section you fall on represents your probability of receiving above-average aid amounts.

one college may not be as attractive to another. For instance, a student that is in the top 20 percent of a graduating class in high school may be a very special candidate for admissions at one college, but merely run-of-the-mill at another school with a more selective admissions process. For this reason, it is critical that you compare award offers only between colleges in the same class or grouping. A review of a school's admissions selectivity in any popular college profile book will help you identify colleges of similar class. One other thing to remember: the college admissions staff will tell you they can't negotiate your aid package. This is not true, but always present your offers from other colleges as casual comments, not as threats.

INSIDER'S ADVICE

HOW TO NEGOTIATE FINANCIAL AID PACKAGES

DO	DON'T
▶ Compare financial aid with same "class" colleges	▶ Act arrogant in presenting aid already offered
▶ Compare the same aid types (don't mix loans with grants)	▶ Turn down one offer until you have another one in writing
▶ Be realistic in your aid expectations	▶ Be impressed with additional loans as aid substitutes
▶ Identify why the college is awarding you aid	▶ Accept a verbal offer for possible aid in your 2nd year of college
▶ Be prepared to make a college choice when offered aid	▶ Lie about other aid
	▶ Present aid demands as an ultimatum

PROFILES

After Reena was accepted at her first college choice, she was pleased to learn that she would be given a leadership scholarship by the college. She was selected based upon her grades, athletic accomplishments, and record of serving in local leadership roles. She soon began to wonder what kind of aid her other college choices might come up with. When talking to the admission staff member at her second college choice, she mentioned the leadership award she had been offered by the first college. They not only matched it but also promised her an additional $3,500 per year.

32.   Collect a Federal Grant

Let Uncle Sam help with your tuition. The federal government awards grants to financially needy students. These grants are not repaid. The largest federal grant program involves PELL grants. The PELL grant maximum award for the neediest students for the 2001–2002 year was $3,750. The government targets Pell grants toward low-income students but provides money on a sliding scale based on family income. Those families with gross income above $50,000 have little chance of receiving Pell Aid. To determine the amount of aid you

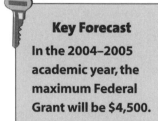

Key Forecast

In the 2004–2005 academic year, the maximum Federal Grant will be $4,500.

can receive from the government, fill out a Free Application for Federal Student Aid (FAFSA) form and submit it to the financial aid office at the colleges you are considering or directly to the government. Based on the data you provide on the FAFSA, the federal government will use a formula to calculate an Estimated Family Contribution (EFC). This is the amount you and your family will be expected to pay toward your education in the next year.

The amount will vary based on whether you are declared a dependent or an independent student (Cost-Saving Strategy 39). It also is impacted by income level, assets owned, family size, and number of family members enrolled in college. Once the EFC is calculated, it remains the same amount for any college you choose, whether tuition is $1,000 or $35,000. However, the EFC calculation represents just a part of the financial plan for your education. It merely helps colleges assess your need for financial aid. This remaining need is referred to as "unmet financial need." The college recognizes that you will need aid to cover this dollar amount.

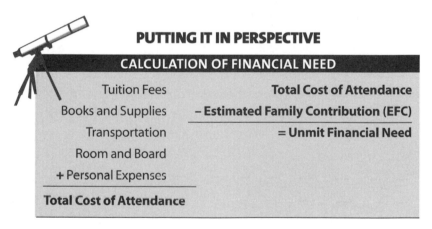

PUTTING IT IN PERSPECTIVE

CALCULATION OF FINANCIAL NEED	
Tuition Fees	**Total Cost of Attendance**
Books and Supplies	**– Estimated Family Contribution (EFC)**
Transportation	**= Unmit Financial Need**
Room and Board	
+ Personal Expenses	
Total Cost of Attendance	

33. Get a Federal Supplemental Grant

The Supplemental Educational Opportunity Grant (SEOG) program complements the Federal PELL Program (Cost-Saving Strategy 32). It is available only to PELL eligible students and is also a grant that does not need to be repaid. SEOG grants go to extremely low-income students; those with the lowest Expected Family Contribution (EFC) as calculated by the federal government's methodology. The awards of up to $780 per/year per student come from federal dollars, but individual colleges award the money at the discretion of the financial aid office. The college receives a lump sum from the federal government, and then gives it to PELL-eligible students based on the school's own formula and aid calendar.

34. Earn a State Grant

Many states have their own program of grant aid that is given directly to students. Like the Federal PELL Grant (Cost-Saving Strategy 32), the state grants are not repaid. Usually these are need-based grants that go to students with unmet need of a certain dollar amount. However, in some states, students not needy enough to qualify for PELL grants receive awards from these state grant programs.

Some states may restrict these funds for use at public colleges and universities, but others make them available to students enrolled at private schools as well. You must attend a college in your state of residence and continue to earn satisfactory grades to receive these awards.

35. Take Out a Federally Subsidized Interest Loan

Most students will have to borrow money to attend college. The largest financial self-help program is named the Stafford Subsidized Loan Program. The "subsidized" in the title refers to the fact that the federal government subsidizes the interest while you attend college. When you leave college, you will repay the loan with interest over a number of years.

The size of your Stafford Subsidized Loan depends upon your need, the college costs, and your year in college (freshman, sophomore, junior, senior). You can calculate basic loan need by subtracting your EFC from the college's cost of attendance, which includes tuition, fees, and room and board if necessary.

> **Stat-to-Know**
>
> **Loans now make up 60% of the average financial aid package.**

For the past ten years, colleges increased tuition much faster than the grant programs have grown. This has forced more students to borrow money and to leave college with average student debt approaching $20,000. These loan programs are essential for many students and provide a very attractive alternative to conventional borrowing. The interest you pay during the repayment period may also be tax deductible.

PUTTING IT IN PERSPECTIVE

SUBSIDIZED STAFFORD LOAN INFORMATION

Eligibility:	Need Based
Who Borrows:	Students
Required Credit Check:	None
Payment begins:	6 months after leaving school
Max. Interest Rate:	8.25% (2000)
Current Annual Rate Charged:	5.39%
Max Loan Year 1:	$2,625
Max Loan Year 2:	$3,500
Max Loan Year 3:	$5,500
Fees Due At Close:	3%

36. Take Out an Unsubsidized Interest Loan

Unsubsidized Stafford Loans are not based on your need. You may receive both a subsidized (Cost-Saving Strategy 35) and an unsubsidized loan during the same enrollment period. The unsubsidized loans are available to independent students and dependent students whose parents do not qualify for the PLUS Loan (Cost-Saving Strategy 37).

The "unsubsidized" name in the title refers to the fact that the government does not pay the interest while you attend school, as is done in the Stafford Subsidized Loan program. You can either begin repayment immediately after securing the funds, or capitalize the interest and begin making payments after you have been out of school for six months. Capitalizing interest simply means the lender will add the interest due while you are in school to the total amount of the loan. This does, however, charge you interest on the interest. For most students, the loan limits are higher for the unsubsidized loans than they are for the subsidized program.

Key Forecast

The class of 2005 will graduate with average debt of $25,000.

37. Use the PLUS Loan for Parents

Parents of dependent students may take out a Federal PLUS Loan to meet the difference between their cost of attendance and other aid the student receives. Borrowers must start repaying these loans within sixty days of disbursement of funds. Parents applying for the PLUS Loan must pass a credit check to determine eligibility. Borrowers can charge a fee of up to 4 percent on these loans. The interest rate changes each year but will not go above 9 percent. You can defer the principal payment and capitalize the interest, rolling the interest into the loan and increasing the total amount of the loan principle.

PUTTING IT IN PERSPECTIVE

COMPARISON OF SUBSIDIZED, UNSUBSIDIZED, AND PARENT LOANS

	PLUS	Subsidized	Unsubsidized
Eligibility:	Not Need Based	Need Based	Not Need Based
Who Borrows:	Parent	Student	Student
Required Credit Check:	Yes	No	No
Payment begins:	Immediately	6 months after leaving school	Immediately
Max. Interest Rate:	9%	8.25%	8.25%
Current Annual Rate Charged:	6.79%	5.39%	5.39%
Max Loan Year 1:	Difference between Cost of Attendance and Other Aid Awarded	$2,625	$4,000
Max Loan Year 2:		$3,500	$4,000
Max Loan Year 3:		$5,500	$5,000
Fees Due At Close:	3%	3%	3%

38. Look into College Work Study (CWS)

As part of your total financial aid package, your college may offer you a work-study position. This need-based program, partially funded by the federal government and partially by the individual college, will pay you a salary for doing an assigned job.

Most work-study positions involve campus jobs, but some programs extend to not-for-profit organizations outside of the college that are approved by the college work-study coordinator. College work-study positions provide much-needed financial assistance and will also give you valuable work experience. The number of hours you can work depends on your financial-need as calculated by the processing of your FAFSA (Free Application for Federal Student Aid).

PUTTING IT IN PERSPECTIVE

FORMULA FOR DETERMINING YOUR ELIGIBILITY FOR COLLEGE WORK STUDY (CWS) PROGRAMS

Total Cost of Attendance
− Estimated Family Contribution (EFC)
= **Financial Need**
− All Other Aid Awards
= **Unmet Need or CWS Eligibility**

You qualify for a work-study job if you have unmet financial need, but need alone will not get you the job. Once eligible, you then must locate a position and apply for it just as you would for any other job. After you land a position, you will receive a regular paycheck. You can spend the money as you wish. After you have earned the amount of your unmet need for the year, you will have to give up your position.

39. Benefit from Your Financial Aid Status

Institutional financial aid, which comes directly from the college, is awarded at least in part based on need. It comes in the form of scholarships or loans. Aid from state and federal sources is heavily need-based. Need is calculated by independent agencies as well as by the college itself (Cost-Saving Strategy 32). When reviewing data for consideration in aid decisions, schools classify a student as either dependent or independent. Dependent students' financial aid depends on their own financial position as well as that of their parents(s) or guardian(s). Dependent students include their parents' income and assets on their financial aid application. Independent students will be evaluated on their own financial position alone. You may be able to get more aid if you wait until you become financially independent before enrolling. This works as long as you don't anticipate having a large annual income while you take classes. The following criteria are almost universally used when determining independent status.

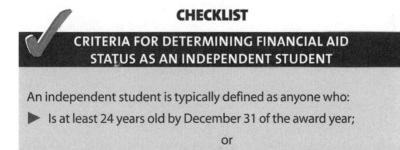

CHECKLIST

CRITERIA FOR DETERMINING FINANCIAL AID STATUS AS AN INDEPENDENT STUDENT

An independent student is typically defined as anyone who:

▶ Is at least 24 years old by December 31 of the award year;

or

▶ Is an orphan or ward of the court;

(Continued)

**CRITERIA FOR DETERMINING FINANCIAL AID
STATUS AS AN INDEPENDENT STUDENT (Continued)**

or

▶ Is a veteran of the Armed Forces of the United States;

or

▶ Is a graduate or professional student;

or

▶ Is a married student;

or

▶ Is a student who has legal dependents other than a spouse;

or

▶ Is a student for whom a financial aid administrator determines and documents independent status on the basis of unusual circumstances.

40. Delay Taking Income to Increase Aid

Don't settle for less financial aid than you are entitled to. You can increase your potential financial aid by managing income flow.

Financial aid calculations take into account assets, debt, income, and the college plans of family members. Aid providers review these items for students and their parents, and students alone when they quality for independent status. Aid formulas use income figures from your and your parent's most recent federal income tax forms. The lower the income level, the more need-based aid that you will qualify for. Any legal means of deferring income in any given year is a good financial aid strategy. Often this is merely a delaying tactic but it can be used to maximize total college aid.

As a dependent student, your parents will want to avoid taking any IRA distributions. They will also want to contribute the maximum to their IRA account. They should also delay bonuses until after the beginning of the new year. If they sell any real estate, they may want to consider an installment sale to avoid recognizing a large gain in one year. Self-employed individuals may wish to take less income, leaving the money in the business. These and other tactics are best used in years when you feel you have unusually high income.

41. Earn Institutional Scholarships for Achievement

Get credit for your special talents. Institutional aid comes in many forms and in greatly varying amounts. A scholarship or institutional aid is financial assistance that comes directly from school funds rather than from government or outside agencies. The college has full control over making these awards. As discussed earlier, financial aid is most often awarded on a need basis, but many schools are beginning to make more awards based upon achievement or performance. This type of aid usually depends on pre-college accomplishments such as high school grades, transfer grades, or standardized test scores. It may also be awarded based upon your grades while at another college or university.

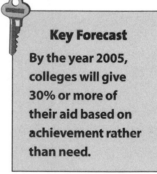

Key Forecast

By the year 2005, colleges will give 30% or more of their aid based on achievement rather than need.

THE WINNERS

COLLEGES WITH A LARGE PERCENTAGE OF THEIR STUDENTS EARNING AWARDS BASED UPON ACHIEVEMENT

State	University
Alaska	University of Alaska-Southwest
California	California Lutheran University
	Westmont College
Colorado	Colorado Christian University
Hawaii	Brigham Young University-Hawaii
Illinois	DePaul University
	Lake Forest College
	Robert Morris College
	Lewis University
Indiana	DePauw University
Mississippi	University of Southern Mississippi
Missouri	University of Missouri-Columbia
New York	Adelphi University
	Cooper Union College
North Carolina	Campbell University
Ohio	Denison University
	Walsh University
Oklahoma	Oklahoma Baptist University
Texas	Houston Baptist University
	Lubbock Christian University
Wisconsin	Lakeland College
	University of Wisconsin-Superior

The chance of earning an achievement-based award will have a lot to do with the competition. You can enhance your chances by attending a community college to bring your GPA up if your high school performance isn't strong. Retaking your ACT or SAT after intensive preparation does not usually change your score dramatically, but if you lie just a point or so away from the cutoff, a retest may help you earn a scholarship. Colleges also give awards to "well-rounded" students who can show a record of leadership, volunteer activity, or special talent in the arts.

42. Earn a National Merit Scholarship™

Every year, thousands of college freshman receive National Merit Scholarships™. These winners receive scholarship dollars from corporations sponsoring the program and from the colleges and universities themselves. The student winners represent the top students in the country; colleges actively recruit them. Having a large number of National Merit Scholars™ attending an institution gives the school added prestige. In fact, the "fight" for these students becomes quite competitive as colleges attempt to climb the rankings ladder by enrolling larger numbers of these scholars. Having lots of these scholars on campus can be more important to a college than

> **Stat-to-Know**
>
> National Merit Scholarship™ winners represent less than 1/2% of all newly enrolled college students.

having a star athlete in terms of attracting top faculty, gifts, and alumni support. Colleges that have the largest numbers of Merit Scholars™ enrolled are often the same schools most highly ranked in the overall rankings of institutions. This is not a coincidence.

43. Earn a State Scholarship for Academic Achievement

Several states award financial aid to recent high school graduates who maintained a certain minimum grade point average (typically a B average) in high school and who agree to attend an in-state college or university, including public universities, community colleges, and private universities.

While the amount of aid available in these programs is small in comparison to the need-based programs that states offer, they seem very generous to the individuals receiving the scholarships. A few of the programs give students full scholarships covering all tuition and fees at any of the state's community colleges or public universities, or a scholarship to private colleges or universities that will cover at least part of the tuition and fees.

INSIDER'S ADVICE

ACHIEVEMENT-BASED STATE SCHOLARSHIPS

▶ Maintain a B or better average in high school

▶ Continue to earn a B or higher average in college

▶ Secure the recommendation of your high school administration

▶ Be a recent high school graduate

▶ Attend a regionally accredited college or university

▶ Attend an in-state college or university

To determine whether or not your state has such a program and whether you are eligible, contact a counselor in the college planning office of your local high school or a representative of the state board of higher education and ask for material explaining the achievement scholarship programs.

44. Earn an Athletic Scholarship

Most high school athletes do not have the ability to play major college sports, especially at the Division I level, which represents the top 300 athletic programs. The good news is that other, very competitive programs allow a great number of athletes to participate. Especially attractive are the opportunities provided by the NAIA (National Association of Intercollegiate Athletics) programs. Many colleges in this association offer scholarships to student athletes in a wide variety of sports. This is especially true in women's sports, for which colleges have rapidly added new opportunities to meet the guidelines initiated by Title IX, a federal directive requiring

> **Stat-to-Know**
>
> Nearly 200,000 women will participate in intercollegiate athletics in 2002.

INSIDER'S ADVICE

HOW TO GO ABOUT EARNING AN ATHLETIC SCHOLARSHIP

▶ Make a highlight film of your varsity experience

▶ Contact the athletic departments of colleges of interest to you

▶ Participate in national camps, festivals, tournaments, and clinics

▶ Inform your high school coaches of your interest in playing at the collegiate level

▶ Meet with athletic recruitment services

▶ Register on Internet sites recommended by your coach for collegiate athletics

▶ Fill out and return the athletic questionnaires sent to you by colleges

that colleges provide equal athletic-scholarship opportunities for both men and women. College athletes often receive aid that covers tuition, books, fees, room and board, or various combinations of these. Aid packages will differ at various competition levels and in different sports.

While athletics at the collegiate level represent a tremendous experience, you should know that your academic life will be different when you participate on a sports team. You will need to become an efficient manager of time, and keep focused on the concept of student first, athlete second.

45. Design an Asset Allocation Strategy

Nearly every college requires that you fill out the Free Application for Federal Student Aid (FAFSA) for every year that you apply for financial aid.

If you are a dependent of your parents, the formula considers both your and your parents' financial positions when determining how much need-based aid you will receive. Currently, children are expected to use up to 35 percent of their available assets to pay for their college expenses, while parents contribute as little as 5.6 percent of theirs. This policy is based on the assumption that parents tend to have a much larger asset pool and that they have many other responsibilities to fund with their assets. In addition, students are expected to pay more

> **Stat-to-Know**
>
> A dependent child is expected to contribute a much larger percentage of their assets toward college costs than their parents are.

because of the direct benefit that they receive in the form of education and awarded financial aid.

By carefully planning for college, a family can make maximum use of this information by controlling the amount of assets owned by the student and making prudent transfers from child to parent. If you own your own business, keep as many assets as possible in the business name.

INSIDER'S ADVICE

BENEFITS OF PARENT VS. DEPENDENT OWNED ASSETS

Parent's Assets	Dependent's Assets
▶ Parents have full control the asset	▶ Dependent usually pays less tax on gain or interest earned
▶ Parents are expected to pay a smaller percentage of their assets for college expenses	▶ Student controls funds at death of parent
▶ If not used for college there is no penalty	▶ Student builds sense of responsibility for use of funds

A less attractive (from a financial aid standpoint) investment asset transfer is from the parent to the child. Each parent can give up to $10,000 per year ($20,000 for a couple) to a child without paying a gift tax on the transfer. This is regulated by the Uniform Gift to Minors Act (UGMA). Parents should know that children under 14 who earn more than $1,400 on those assets will pay tax at the parents' rate. You can avoid this hit by keeping the money in mutual funds or stocks and not cashing out until the child turns 14. Once the child reaches 14 years of age, all gains are taxed at the child's presumably lower rate. This is one of the least attractive of the investment options because it is taxable and is totally controlled by the child upon reaching the age of consent.

CHAPTER 6

Utilize Savings and Tax Breaks

The surest way to control college costs is to begin saving early through a number of special programs designed for college savings and to take advantage of the tax breaks available to students and their families.

46. Investigate the Hope Tax Credit

Don't miss out on this tax break. The Tax Relief Act retained the Hope Tax Credit for individuals attending college or paying for someone else in their family to attend. This after-the-fact tax break provides a great way to cut your college costs. The Hope Tax Credit is not a tax deduction, but is subtracted directly from the total tax liability. You can earn the tax credit of up to $1,500 during each of the first two years of undergraduate study. Any number of individuals in a family may use this credit during the same year. The Hope Tax Credit allows you to take a credit for the first $1,000 of eligible expenses paid during the year for required tuition and fees. You may then take 50 percent of the next $1,000 spent in the same period, for a total of $1,500, per year/per student.

CHECKLIST

REQUIREMENTS FOR THE HOPE TAX CREDIT

▶ You must owe tax during the year that credit is taken

▶ The student must be the taxpayer, spouse, or dependent of the taxpayer

▶ You must not be claimed by anyone else

▶ Have income of under $100,000 if filing a joint return

▶ Have income of under $50,000 if filing a single return

▶ Be enrolled at least part-time in college

▶ Be enrolled in the first two years of college

▶ Be enrolled in a college that is eligible for federal student financial aid programs

▶ Can be used only for tuition and fees

47. Take the Lifetime Learning Tax Credit

> **Stat-to-Know**
>
> The Lifetime Learning Tax Credit covers up to 20 percent of the first $5,000 spent on tuition.

This Lifetime Learning Tax Credit provides another tax-savings opportunity. Families may earn a total tax credit of up to $2,000 per family, which is subtracted from their tax liability. The program covers tuition and fees for everyone in the family, up to 20 percent of the first $5,000 spent. You cannot combine both the Lifetime Learning Tax Credit and the Hope Tax Credit (Cost-Saving Strategy 46) in the same tax year. The Lifetime Learning Tax

Credit is more comprehensive because it covers expenses beyond just the first two years of study. Consider taking the Hope Credit first since it only covers the first two years. Families can take this credit for as many years as they pay qualifying expenses.

CHECKLIST

REQUIREMENTS FOR THE LIFETIME LEARNING TAX CREDIT

▶ You must owe tax during the year that credit is required

▶ The student must be the taxpayer, spouse, or dependent of the taxpayer

▶ You must not be claimed by anyone else

▶ Have income of under $100,000 if filing a joint return

▶ Have income of under $50,000 if filing a single return

▶ Be enrolled at least part-time in college

▶ You can be in any year of college (graduate or undergraduate)

▶ Be enrolled in a college eligible for federal student financial aid programs

▶ Can be used only for tuition and fees

▶ After the year 2002, the credit will increase to 20% of the first $10,000.

48. Deduct Educational Loan Interest

In 2002 and 2003, taxpayers can deduct up to $3,000 per year of loan interest as an adjustment to income. For 2004 and 2005, the amount will

Key Forecast

There will be a considerable increase in the cap allowed for this deduction after 2005.

go up to $4,000. You can take this deduction even if you do not itemize. The borrowed funds must have been used for education, and only the individual taking out the loan can take the deduction. If parents claim the student as a dependent for tax purposes, then the parents must be responsible for the loan in order to get the deduction. The benefit phases out at certain levels of income. The deduction cannot be taken in years in which the Hope or Lifetime Learning Credit are taken. The IRS has approved tuition, fees, books, room and board, and transportation as allowable deductions for tax purposes.

49. Check out the New Education IRAs

If you have several years to save for someone's college education, Education IRAs or Education Savings Accounts as they are now named, make a good savings tool. Families may deposit up to $2,000 a year of after-tax dollars into an account for each child in the family under the age of eighteen. You can set up these accounts through any financial institution. You pay no tax as the money earns interest, and pay no tax when you take the money out and use it for school expenses. It actually can be used for any educational expenses

Key Forecast

In the next four years, the maximum annual amount allowed for deposit in an Education IRA will increase to $5,000.

from kindergarten through college. While the Internal Revenue Service phases out the benefit for higher-income families, it does provide a nice vehicle through which people can accumulate funds for children as they grow up. In many families, parents or grandparents contribute to these funds on an annual basis, such as on a child's birthday.

You can invest the Education IRA in any vehicle used for a regular IRA and need specify no education use designation when you fund the account. When you set up the account, establish it in the name of the child whose college expenses it will fund. If the child has not used all the funds by the time he or she reaches the age of 30, the account must be closed or transferred to a younger member of the family. This benefit phases out for individuals with adjusted gross income between $95,000 and $110,000. It phases out for married couples with income between $190,000 and $220,000.

50. Save Now for College Later

Many college students with their own children feel the double pressure of paying for their own college and providing for their children's future educational needs. Five years at a college that costs $30,000 a year in 2002 will probably cost more than $230,000 in total for a student who begins in the year 2015. And that is a conservative

Key Forecast

Over the next decade, college costs will increase at three times the savings interest rate.

estimate! If you earn 7 percent on your savings, you will need to put away $10,505 per year, or $1,875 per month, in today's dollars to cover that total cost. The glory of compounding interest will help you cover college costs in the future. Start saving for college now.

DOLLARS AND SENSE

		Amount		
Year	Age	Needed To Save	College Expenditures	Total Savings
2002	5	$10,505	$0	$10,505
2003	6	$10,505	$0	$21,745
2004	7	$10,505	$0	$33,772
2005	8	$10,505	$0	$46,641
2006	9	$10,505	$0	$60,410
2007	10	$10,505	$0	$75,144
2008	11	$10,505	$0	$90,909
2009	12	$10,505	$0	$107,777
2010	13	$10,505	$0	$125,826
2011	14	$10,505	$0	$145,139
2012	15	$10,505	$0	$165,803
2013	16	$10,505	$0	$187,914
2014	17	$10,505	$0	$211,573
2015	18	$10,505	$56,569	$180,318
2016	19	$10,505	$59,398	$144,047
2017	20	$10,505	$62,368	$102,268
2018	21	$10,505	$65,486	$54,445
2019	22	$10,505	$68,761	$0

The table header spans: **SAVINGS FOR A 5-YEAR-OLD'S COLLEGE EDUCATION**

Saving for college now will translate into tremendous savings in total college costs by allowing you to take out fewer student loans. The interest savings if you don't use loans can be enormous.

DOLLARS AND SENSE

LOAN VS. SAVINGS		
	Loan Plan*	Savings Plan**
Amount Needed for College	$100,000	$100,000
10-yr Monthly Payment Amount	$1,266	$528.00
Total Amount You Will Pay Over 10 Years	$151,920	$63,360

*Assumes a 9% interest charge on loan.

** Assumes a 5% growth rate on savings.

51. Buy U.S. Savings Bonds

One almost risk-free way to save for college is with Series EE or I, U.S. Savings Bonds. While the rules for qualifying for tax exemption with savings bonds look complex, they really aren't. These instruments offer an attractive alternative for families. The interest earned on the bonds becomes fully tax-exempt at redemption if used for educational purposes by a family with adjusted gross income below a certain level. The rate of interest that these bonds earn changes every six months. They currently pay a rate equivalent to more than 8 percent when compared with taxable instruments.

52. Lock-in Tuition Rates with Prepaid Tuition Plans (Section 529)

The cost of going to college is increasing at more than twice the rate of inflation. Each year, the average family must use a larger share of its earnings to pay annual tuition and fees.

Today's newborn will pay three times today's total college costs. A number of states recognize this problem and have set up prepaid programs that allow families to pay at today's prices to lock in college tuition for the future. You are actually buying a tuition contract from the state. You fund the program at today's tuition rates and get protection from all of the tuition increases that will occur between today and the start of college for your child. In some states, these programs only cover public colleges and universities in that state.

However, most states allow you to use the funds for college expenses at public or private colleges, at in-state and out-of-state institutions. The private college tuition is guaranteed at the average public college tuition increase over the life of the investment.

CHECKLIST
POINTS TO EXPLORE WHEN SELECTING A PREPAID TUITION PLAN

▶ Who can participate in the program?

▶ How will it impact your financial aid?

▶ How to fund—monthly, yearly, or lump sum?

▶ At what colleges can it be used?

▶ What happens if the child does not go to college?

▶ Are there any age restrictions on the use of this program?

▶ Can the money be used at private institutions?

Under Section 529 of the tax code, the earnings on these funds are totally tax-free when the money is used to pay for qualified education expenses. Be aware that these plans will reduce your eligibility for federal financial aid. Every state program works differently, so you need to investigate before selecting one.

53. Discover State-Sponsored "529" Investment Plans

In these plans, named after Section 529 of the 1997 revised tax code, anyone can put away more than $100,000 per child. There is no minimum qualifying deposit. The money grows tax deferred, and at withdrawal is free of federal tax if used for qualifying education expenses.

Most states sponsor these programs and open them to both in-state and out-of-state participants. As an added benefit, resident investors in some states may treat the deposit amount as a tax deduction on state returns.

If a child decides not to attend college or earns a scholarship and doesn't need the money, you can transfer the account to another family member. This family member can even be as distant as a cousin. However, you must eventually use the money for college expenses. If you don't, the funds will be taxed and you will also pay a penalty.

Most states hire large investment companies to administer the plans. You usually have only a couple of choices for investment vehicles. In some cases, the state sets up the funding so that older children have their money in less-risky investments. Just as with any financial investment, you should study carefully the state funds that interest you.

INSIDER'S ADVICE

WHAT TO LOOK FOR WHEN CONSIDERING "529" STATE INVESTMENT PLANS.

▶ Return history for the fund over at least a three year period

▶ Amount of annual expenses charged

▶ How many investment choices does the program allow

▶ Can the investment vehicle be changed as the child gets older

▶ What is the management firm's overall record for all investments

Remember that you can select just about any state's program and use it at the college or university of your choice. It doesn't matter where you live or where your college choice is located. The amount of income earned on these investments is tax-free but will be treated as income of the student for aid evaulation purposes. This will reduce any financial aid awards that are need based as students are expected to use 50 percent of their annual income to pay for education.

54. Investigate State College Savings Bonds

Some states offer zero-coupon bonds as a college savings vehicle. "Zero-coupon" simply means that bondholders receive no annual interest. The bond earns its interest at the date of maturity. These investments are bonds with a face value of a certain dollar amount, say $5,000, that you purchase for less than that face value. The bond appreciates in value as it matures. The amount needed to purchase the bonds will vary depending on the number of years left until you plan to use the proceeds for college expenses. Gains on these bonds are exempt from both state and federal taxes and may pay you an added state-funded bonus if you use them for tuition and fees at an in-state college or university.

These bonds are actually known as municipal bonds. They generally carry low risk and offer decent rates of return. Families in higher tax brackets will realize a higher return on the bonds because of the greater amount of tax savings at their higher tax bracket. The bond's proceeds usually won't reduce state financial aid awards. Individuals may purchase only a specified amount of these bonds.

DOLLARS AND SENSE

CURRENT PRICE OF STATE BONDS

$5,000 bonds maturing on this year:	Cost this much in: January 2002
2005	$4,413.90
2006	4,214.30
2007	4,020.55
2008	3,830.60
2009	3,643.60
2010	3,461.70
2011	3,285.05
2012	3,113.75
2017	2,290.85
2018	2,149.75
2019	2,021.25
2020	1,898.55
2021	1,784.85
2022	1,679.85
2023	1,580.15
2024	1,488.60

CHAPTER 7

Find College Money in Other Sources

L
et someone else pay your college expenses. If you are willing to give a service, there are many organizations that will financially support your college education. This section reviews the best ways to secure this type of assistance.

55. Find a Company That Will Pay Your Tuition

Key Forecast

By 2005, corporate America will spend nearly $15 billion on tuition reimbursement each year.

Finding companies that will pay your tuition as an employee is easier than you might think. Last year, corporate America spent nearly $13 billion on the college education expenses of their employees. More than 8 million college students work full time while pursuing degrees on a part-time basis, and a large share of them get tuition reimbursement at work.

Combining work and education really is a positive experience for both the employee and the employer. Economists estimate that for every $1 a company spends on tuition reimbursement, it receives $10 to $15 back in benefits tied to the new skills and the increased productivity that their employees bring to their jobs.

Fifty years ago, tuition reimbursement was considered an unusual benefit. But today, about three out of every four companies offer some sort of tuition reimbursement program. Many companies offer this benefit because it helps them attract and retain people

THE WINNERS
COMPANIES WITH GENEROUS TUITION REIMBURSEMENT

American Management Systems, Inc.

American Tobacco Company

BellSouth Communication Systems

Boeing

Burlington Industries

Capital One Financial Corp.

Carilion Health System

Coors Brewing Company

DuPont

DynCorp

Eastman Chemical Comp

Elizabeth Arden

Federal Reserve Bank

Fleet Bank

General Electric

Hamilton Beach/Proctor-Silex

Lucent Technologies

Nationwide Insurance

Nokia Corp.

Phillip Morris Reynolds Company

RR Donnelley & Sons Company

Salomon Smith Barney

Sears

State Farm Insurance Company

U.S. Cellular Corp.

U.S. Postal Service

Verizon Communications

Westvaco

in a competitive job market. Employees find tuition reimbursement critical and consider it a positive reason for joining an organization. In a recent survey that I completed of 550 human resources officers in large metropolitan areas, tuition reimbursement was reported as the most requested benefit of new employees. Companies have responded to this demand by improving and expanding the benefits that these programs offer.

PROFILES

Sandy was a twenty-one-year-old with 64 hours of college credits from courses she completed at the local community college. She started working for a large firm as an office assistant in the marketing department. After one year, she felt she had little opportunity to grow with the firm and enrolled at an area college on a part-time basis. She was delighted to learn that her company was willing to reimburse her for her college costs. This included tuition, books, fees, and a transportation stipend. All she had to do was stay employed with the firm while in college and maintain a B-average in her coursework. She took so many courses that her reimbursement exceeded the allowed IRS tax-free maximum by several hundred dollars, which she gladly paid taxes on. In four years, she was able to finish her degree and looks forward to advancement in her company.

While many companies offer tuition assistance, the benefits take different forms. You should always ask a potential employer how its program works before you take the job. Some companies, for instance, may require specific length-of-service terms before they'll reimburse your tuition. That's very important to know if you plan to fund college through these benefits. Also remember that the Internal Revenue Service allows your tuition reimbursement benefit to be tax-free up to $5,250 per year if the training directly relates to your current position, not some future promotion. That means that any reimbursement you receive over this amount in a single year will be treated as additional income for tax purposes. Politicians in Washington have talked about raising this limit, and there is a good chance it will happen soon.

INSIDER'S ADVICE

COMMON POLICIES RELATED TO TUITION REIMBURSEMENT PROGRAMS

▶ The annual dollar amount will be capped

▶ Reimbursement will be for tuition and mandatory fees

▶ The amount of reimbursement may be tied to the grade that you earn

▶ The specific course of study will have to be approved

▶ You will be required to have six months to a year of service before being entitled to the benefit

▶ You may be expected to sign an agreement to stay with the organization for a certain period of time

▶ You must attend a regionally accredited institution.

▶ The reimbursement may be treated as a loan that you "write-off" through future employment

Many industries provide tuition reimbursement, but these programs are most often found in information technology, telecommunications, and manufacturing. In fields where workers need significant academic credentials before they are hired, such as education and health fields, the benefit is less common or given in smaller amounts. Not-for-profit and smaller organizations with limited budgets may offer such programs, but benefits will usually be much smaller than those offered at major for-profit corporations.

If you receive six years of reimbursement and invest it for your retirement, that money can pay big dividends both now and in the future.

DOLLARS AND SENSE

FUTURE VALUE OF TUITION REIMBURSEMENT

Six years of Average Reimbursement	Invested Value of Reimbursement Over:		
	10 years	20 years	40 years
$10,000	$21,589.25	$46,609.57	$217,245.21
$15,000	$32,383.87	$69,914.36	$325,867.82
$20,000	$43,178.50	$93,219.14	$434,490.43

56. Find Work at a College

Many colleges offer their employees discounted or free tuition as a benefit of working at the school. If a student has the patience and persistence to secure a job at such an institution or its related hospital, athletic department, or development office, the savings can be tremendous. Often

Stat-to-Know

Colleges and universities are one of America's largest employers.

such benefits can be extended into graduate study. To take full advantage of these programs, you must become a full-time employee before your initial enrollment. Not only will you save money, but you will also gain valuable work experience and earn a living.

A generous tuition reimbursement program will allow you to take several courses a term, charge you only for registration fees, provide an unlimited number of terms of study, cover all majors and provide for graduate level study.

THE WINNERS

COLLEGES THAT HAVE A GENEROUS TUITION REIMBURSEMENT POLICY FOR THEIR EMPLOYEES.

State	University
Arkansas	University of Arkansas–Main Campus
California	United States International University
District of Columbia	Howard University Southeastern University
Florida	Rollins College
Georgia	Georgia Institute of Technology
Illinois	DePaul University Loyola University-Chicago North Park University Robert Morris College Southern Illinois University
Iowa	Eastern Iowa Community College
Maryland	College of Notre Dame of Maryland Johns Hopkins University

State	University
Massachusetts	Fitchburg State College
	Springfield College
Minnesota	College of St. Catherine
	St. Olaf College
Missouri	Central Missouri State University
Nebraska	University of Nebraska
New Jersey	Montclair State University
New York	Bank Street College
	Clarkson University
	Hamilton College
	Iona College
	Le Moyne College
	New York University
	Pace University
	Regents College
Ohio	Denison University
	Kent State University
	Miami University-Oxford
	University of Dayton
	Cuyahoga College
	University of Rio Grande
	Hocking College
Pennsylvania	Dickinson College
	Harrisburg Area Community College
	Widener University
Texas	Trinity University
Virgin Islands	University of the Virgin Islands
Washington	St. Martin's College
	University of Puget Sound
	Washington State University
West Virginia	College of West Virginia
Wisconsin	University of Wisconsin System

To find a job at a college contact the college Human Resources office and ask for a list of openings, and then review the employee handbook section on the tuition waiver policy before enrolling. Be sure not to confuse work-study jobs with full-time employment.

57. Attend a Bible College

You don't have to be holy to attend a bible college. While not for everyone, Bible colleges often present an excellent choice for some students. Some of these colleges only offer programs related to religion or theology. However, they often have much broader offerings, particularly at schools with a religious heritage that does not include a mandate to educate clergy. Programs related to religion might include pastoral counseling, ministry, mission work, church music, religious education, evangelism, Bible studies, comparative religion, church management, or even missionary aviation.

These colleges often receive financial support from churches of their denomination as well as direct support from individuals and then pass it on to students. Often individual churches will send students and support their education. Other schools will give a free education to any member of their faith. Bible colleges range from small, correspondence-based programs to large institutions with a wide range of nonreligious programs. However, even these schools usually have a flavor and atmosphere that clearly defines the colleges as Bible schools.

THE WINNERS

BIBLE COLLEGES	
State	*University*
Alabama	Heritage Christian University
Arizona	Southwestern College

State	University
California	San Jose Christian College
Colorado	Nazarene Bible College
Florida	Hobe Sound Bible College
Georgia	Beulah Heights Bible College
Idaho	Boise Bible College
Illinois	Moody Bible Institute
Iowa	Faith Baptist Bible College
	Vennard College
Kentucky	Clear Creek Baptist Bible College
Michigan	Grace Bible College
Minnesota	Minnesota Bible College
Mississippi	Magnolia Bible College
	Wesley College
Missouri	Saint Louis Christian College
New Mexico	Nazarene Indian Bible College
New York	Practical Bible College
North Carolina	John Wesley College
Ohio	God's Bible School and College
Pennsylvania	Valley Forge Christian College
Tennessee	American Baptist College
	Free Will Baptist Bible College
Texas	Arlington Baptist College
	College of Biblical Studies-Houston
	Rio Grande Bible Institute

PROFILES

Melvin wanted to work in third world countries helping people. When he learned that his church would sponsor him in mission training at a nearby bible college, he was thrilled. The coursework covered studies of culture, geography, ministry, counseling, and even survival. It turned out to be the perfect education for him and a fantastic financial deal.

---

58. Establish State Residency

You don't have to be born in a particular state to become a resident of that state. You can earn state residency before enrolling at a college and pay a reduced tuition rate. State residents pay anywhere from 10 to 100 percent less tuition than out-of-state students at public universities. Private colleges are not considered here because they charge both in-state and out-of-state students the same rate. Many colleges have fairly lenient residency requirements defining who will qualify for in-state tuition rates. These "test" requirements vary from college to college and often require that students meet only one condition of residency to qualify as a state resident for tuition rate purposes.

Stat-to-Know

Students that are state residents pay on average 50% less tuition when attending public universities.

Residency requirements will vary from college to college. They will be easy to meet at some public schools where you merely need to get an in-state driver's license or pay state income taxes.

In other states, you may need to have an address for two years before enrolling.

If you plan to establish residency, you should call the public university of interest and ask for a copy of the in-state residency requirements. College staff may tell you that you cannot esbtablish residency; don't take their word for it. Review the catalog for details. It will present you with a clear legal definition.

THE WINNERS

COLLEGES THAT HAVE "EASY-TO-MEET" RESIDENCY REQUIREMENTS

State	University
Arizona	Arizona State University
California	San Diego State University
Colorado	Colorado State University
Florida	Florida State University
Georgia	Georgia State University
Idaho	Idaho State University
Illinois	Illinois State University
Indiana	Ball State University
	Indiana State University
Iowa	Iowa State University
Kansas	Kansas State University

(Continued)

COLLEGES THAT HAVE "EASY-TO-MEET" RESIDENCY REQUIREMENTS (Continued)	
State	*University*
Kentucky	Murray State University
Louisiana	Louisiana State University-Baton Rouge
Michigan	Michigan State University
Mississippi	Mississippi State University
Montana	Montana State University
New Mexico	New Mexico State University
New York	SUNY
North Carolina	North Carolina State University
North Dakota	North Dakota State University
Ohio	Bowling Green State University
	Kent State University
	Ohio State University
Oklahoma	Oklahoma State University
Oregon	Oregon State University
	Portland State University
Pennsylvania	Pennsylvania State-University Park
Tennessee	Middle Tennessee State University
Utah	Utah State University
Washington	Washington State University

59. Check for Extended Billing Options

Just as you can with every other purchase, you can usually extend your college payments over time. Nearly all colleges have some form of installment billing—you will usually have to pay interest for the privilege of using this payment option, just as you do with a credit card, though some schools give you extended billing options without adding interest. Typically, colleges break payments down to one-third due at registration, one-third before the midpoint of the semester, and one-third before the final weeks of the term. Extended billing programs save on the loan interest of student loans and spread the cash payment load. Some will even spread a full year's worth of tuition over several terms, thus evening out your expenses. If you receive more aid in one term, the college will often even out the amount you owe each month with billing. A college-sponsored billing option will cost you less than the interest charges accrued when using credit cards to pay for college expenses.

> **Stat-to-Know**
>
> It is not unusual for students to spend $5,000 to $10,000 in interest expense on credit cards and extended billing options to cover their college costs.

60. Plan for Student Loan Forgiveness

Perkins loans are federal loans made directly from the institution on a revolving basis. They are attractive because they can be forgiven in total or part for service to society after graduation. You can get a list of the areas of service that will qualify for this forgiveness from your financial aid advisor at the time that you agree to take a Perkins loan as part of your financial aid package. These forgiveness programs were established to encourage college graduates to serve in areas of critical need. As the nation's needs change, so do the specific areas covered by this program.

CHECKLIST

TYPES OF SOCIAL SERVICE THAT QUALIFY BORROWER FOR LOAN FORGIVENESS

▶ Teachers in certain disciplines

▶ Teachers working in certain geographic locations

▶ Social Service workers in high-risk programs

▶ Law enforcement personnel

▶ Peace Corps volunteers

▶ Military Personnel

▶ Nurses

PROFILES

Winnie wanted to find a way to give back after graduation. Her first choice was to go into the Peace Corps. As a twenty-year-old still living at home, she had the freedom to go. However, she thought she couldn't go because of her debt load, until she learned from her college's loan counseling program that her loans could be forgiven for social service of this type.

61. Become a Resident Adviser

If you live on campus, you will probably have the opportunity to apply to be a resident adviser or mentor. These positions will require some of your time and energy. In exchange, they provide you free room and often, free meal programs. You may also receive a stipend and sometimes other discounts on campus. You can easily save $20,000 or more on your college costs in one of these programs.

Some students consider this a great job because it fits well into dorm life. You will have to advise, direct, and counsel other students in the dorm. You don't need any special background. Colleges offer excellent training programs, which will also give you an additional skill set to enhance your resume.

Students who serve as resident advisers can demonstrate that they have held positions of responsibility. They can emphasize their "people skills" and their ability to work cooperatively with others. While the hours you work will cut into your own time, so will those of any other job. And most jobs are not as convenient. If you work as a resident advisor, plan to come to campus before terms begin and be prepared to work weekends and evenings.

62. Work While in College

Finding a job is probably the oldest way for students to help pay college expenses. You may find it difficult to juggle school and work, but most colleges have designed their programs so that they fit a working schedule. Colleges tend to be located in areas that support and

> **Stat-to-Know**
>
> 75% of college students work while in school.

service businesses, which provide job opportunities even on small college town campuses. Many of these jobs may not be great, but they pay the bills.

This is another good reason to attend college in a city. Cities have a range of opportunities so broad that you can find work that not only pays a decent wage, but also has the added benefit of enhancing your education. It is also good for your resume. In recent years, students have developed small businesses of their own while attending college.

You will hear success stories of college students who started companies that sell used books, post party information, arrange trips during breaks, match up students for dates, or provide entertainment services through dot-com companies. College life lends itself to entrepreneurship, because campuses often have a large number of intelligent, creative people with technological skills. Colleges also provide an open forum for sharing ideas, personal computer equipment, and access to information resources all of which are necessary for startup companies.

Regardless of the type of job you find, you must stay focused on your education and design a course schedule that allows for both academics and work.

63. Group Discounts

If you work full time, you can often get a tuition discount if you and several others from your organization enroll in the same program at a college or university. Some schools will actually offer the coursework at your company's location. They will often run these programs on accelerated timetables that are convenient to your work schedule. These programs come in

Key Forecast

Most colleges will develop special programs for employers.

two basic varieties: very specialized education to meet a specific need of your employer or general-studies programs that allow for enrollment of students from a wide variety of interest areas.

INSIDER'S ADVICE

HOW TO GET A GROUP DISCOUNT

▶ Approach coworkers about going to college

▶ Find colleges that have programs in place with other companies

▶ Meet with your Human Resources Department and propose the program and possible colleges

▶ Have the Human Resources Department contact area colleges to determine compatability

▶ Meet as a group with college personnel

▶ Have Human Resources negotiate a special tuition rate and payment plan for the program

64. Earn Student Discounts

Many service companies extend special discount offers to students. These discounts are offered for small dollar amounts to students in the same way that senior citizens are given discounts. Sometimes, you can receive a more substantial benefit in the form of products or services if you maintain a specified grade-point average. Such deals come in the form of cheaper auto insurance, travel rates, lodging costs, auto prices, computer prices, and general credit card rates.

When investigating these programs, make sure you verify for yourself that the rate offered is significantly better than that given to the general public.

65. Join the Armed Forces and Go to College

The No. 1 reason people join the armed forces is education. All of the armed forces (Army, Navy, Air Force, Marines) offer tuition-assistance programs to members on active duty. Recruiters often tout these benefits as one of the primary reasons for enlisting and reenlisting in the service. The aid allows officers and enlisted personnel to take coursework during off-duty time at a college or university on base, in the local area, or through distance-learning programs. The tuition-assistance program pays for college level work earned toward a certificate, associate's, bachelor's, master's, professional, or doctoral degree.

Stat-to-Know

You can get more than half of your college paid for through military service programs.

The military used to advertise that new recruits could join the service and later attend college. Now you can join the service and go to college all at the same time. This is why it makes little sense for anyone to say they are primarily going away to college to "mature." A better choice for these people would be to join the military and "mature" while they travel, grow, take college coursework, and get paid a salary with benefits. The military tuition-assistance programs will pay up to $3,500 per year in tuition for approved schooling.

In order to receive these benefits and have them work toward a degree, you will need good advising (which the military provides) and a little luck so that everything fits together.

Colleges tend to have a lot of respect for military training programs and like the generosity they offer. Shrewd use of this kind of tuition assistance can definitely pay off for students interested in military service.

PUTTING IT IN PERSPECTIVE

PROGRAMS FOR MILITARY BASED TUITION ASSISTANCE

Program	When	Type of Education	Realistic Potential for Credits Earned
Tuition Assistance (TA)	While enlisted	Basic Degree Requirements	36
Formal Military Based Training	While enlisted	Specialized Training Later Converted to College Credit	18
Military College	While enlisted	College Courses Offered by the Military	12
College or University Benefits (MGIB) (Cost-Saving Strategy 66)	After discharge	Completion of College Degree at a College or University	64

CHECK LIST

TO QUALIFY FOR TA BENEFITS

▶ Enroll in accredited program (Cost-Saving Strategy 73)

▶ Work for a new degree or certificate

▶ Receive approval from Military College Planning Office

▶ Successfully complete courses

▶ Have a total educational goal planned

▶ Be on active duty while enrolled

▶ Pay your own fees and book charges

▶ Be enrolled during off-duty time

66. Collect the G.I. Bill

As a veteran of active or reserve duty, you qualify for educational benefits under a program named the Montgomery G.I. Bill, or "MGIB" for short.

The program pays varying amounts based on when and how long you served. Aid also depends on the type of program you pursue and your educational enrollment status (full time, part time, etc.) The benefit pays a monthly stipend that may vary from a couple of thousand dollars per year to more than $10,000 per year. The military typically pays these benefits for up to thirty-six months of education and makes this money available to veterans for up to ten years after their honorable discharge. Individual states also provide programs for veterans, and some colleges give veterans additional scholarship or grant benefits.

INSIDER'S ADVICE

**ITEMS TO LOOK FOR IN A
VETERAN'S CHOICE OF A COLLEGE**

▶ Acceptance of military training for some college credit

▶ Special veterans' advisors

▶ A veterans' club or group

▶ Institution-based veterans' scholarships

▶ Veterans' special job search assistance while enrolled

▶ Veterans' counseling and tutoring center

▶ Veterans' financial aid counselors

Veterans receive other related benefits that fall under the MGIB program. These include special "banked" educational dollars contributed to an account in their name for each month of active duty.

Dependents, including spouses of disabled or killed military personnel, can also receive educational benefits under the MGIB.

PROFILES

James received grants and loans to work toward his degree after his discharge from the Navy. His concern was covering his living expenses. The MGIB program was a savior. He received a monthly stipend on top of his other financial aid. His college of choice also gave him a veterans' discount that he had not expected. Once he started, he figured he could earn his degree in the thirty-six-month window of available MGIB benefits because his college gave him course credit for the technical training he received in the Navy. That credit, added to the credit allowed for the few courses he had completed at the local community college while in the Navy, gave him enough credit to start school as a sophomore.

---

67. Join ROTC

ROTC (Reserve Officer Training Corps) programs were established to assist the service academies in providing officer candidates for active and reserve duty in the United States Army, Navy, and Air Force. The military programs become an integral part of your college education, but allow you to earn your college degree in almost any field.

You can apply for these programs before or after you start college. You may enter the program and pay your own tuition at first or apply for a scholarship before starting. Scholarship winners will usually receive free tuition, fees, and books. They will also receive a monthly allowance or stipend for other expenses. Some college-based programs will also pay your room and board, not as part of the government benefit but as direct aid from the college.

In return for the financial assistance, graduates of ROTC programs will be obligated to a period of service as officers in the United States armed forces. You can usually choose to fulfill this requirement through active duty or reserve status.

SELECTION CRITERIA REVIEWED IN AWARDING ROTC SCHOLARSHIPS

▶ National Honor Society Membership

▶ Better than average college admission test scores

▶ Participation in varsity athletics

▶ Participation in student activities

▶ Student body leadership positions

▶ High school ROTC program participant

▶ Commitment to military service

CHAPTER 8

Get More Immediate Value for Your Dollar

I n this section the strategies focus on the quality of education delivered. These strategies serve as a yardstick for measuring the value of your education, pure and simple. Just as with any other purchases you make, you should expect to receive a quality product from the college you attend.

68. Remember Who Pays Your Tuition

At community colleges and public universities, your tuition only covers a small percent of what the institution spends on your education. Most of the remainder is covered by state, federal, and local community appropriations taken from tax sources. In comparison, private not-for-profit colleges fund about half of your education through sources other than your tuition dollar. At colleges run as for-profit businesses (proprietary schools), you pay more than the actual cost of your education because for-profit colleges use part of your tuition to pay investors/owners profits and to cover income taxes. Before you enroll in an institute, school, or college, make sure to find out if it is a proprietary school. Not all proprietary schools are bad choices, but they do spend less on your education then private not-for-profit and public colleges or universities. Public universities are such great deals because so much of your tuition—about $8,000 per year—is paid by others.

69. Education for Tomorrow

As you look to your future, start by considering what you are preparing for while in college. Are you focusing on your place in the world of 2005 or the world of 2035? The speed of change in the world increases geometrically, and the world of 2035 will look quite different from the one of 2005.

Tomorrow's college graduates must prepare for a world of work in which they will find one constant. This constant is change. That world will be made up of organizations that continually reinvent themselves. People will move freely in and out of jobs and careers. They will enjoy more leisure time and often have shorter careers, but longer lives. This will result in more workers turning to community-service opportunities after retirement.

Work schedules will become more flexible, while jobs themselves will depend less on location and more on the capabilities of the worker. People will need job skills that adapt to new problem sets. Most workers will make several career changes, and education will become a continual process.

Nobody can predict the future, but what we see of it now points to an exciting time in which to live. Finding the right college to help you prepare for this new world can be a huge undertaking. Attempting to guess what the job market will offer in the next few

INSIDER'S ADVICE

COMPARISON OF SKILLS DEVELOPED IN COLLEGE

FUTURE	PAST
▶ *Mining of Information—* The searching, categorizing, analyzing, and reporting of information.	▶ *Research And Analysis—* The development of skills necessary to conduct research to develop "new" information.
▶ *Information Relationship Building*—How information is linked and what these links mean.	▶ *The Imparting of Factual Knowledge*—The collection of information from faculty experts.
▶ *Application of Information to Current Issues*—How information relates to real world situations.	▶ *Formula Approach to Problem Solving*—The memorization of formulas and calculations.
▶ *Application of Information to Problem Solving*—Finding ways to use information to solve case problems.	▶ *Value and Attitude Development*—The building of personal views on issues.
▶ *Creation or Discovery of New Insights*—Developing new insights by combining information sources to solve new, real world issues and concerns.	▶ *Enculturation Into Common Tradition*—As accepted by the majority.
▶ *Ability to Articulate to Others*—Being able to express what has been discovered.	▶ *Life Planning Skills*—Based upon the institutional philosophy.
	▶ *Religious Training*—In the college's faith base.

years seems like an intimidating task, but it is critical as you plan for your future. You can begin preparing for tomorrow's world by making the right college choice today.

Many careers require skills best developed through several different majors, and no single course of study will teach them all. For that reason, you must make smart choices when selecting courses outside of your major. The chart on the previous page highlights the type of education best suited for the future and compares it with educational goals of the past.

When you visit a college campus, spend some time visiting classes and talking to students. Try to determine if the approach to teaching is building for the past or for the future. Look for academic programs that have a technology component in every course.

Planning your education to satisfy the world's job needs is an iffy proposition even when you are just looking at next year. Prognosticating for the year 2035 is even more difficult. Yet, certain future employer needs are fairly apparent. They are actual groups of objectives called skill sets.

These new skill sets fall into two broad groupings—information tasks and creative tasks. Each of the six areas included has both information elements and some creative elements, yet each skill set tends to lean more heavily in either one direction or the other. (See chart on p. 137.)

70. Seek Outcomes

Most of today's jobs already require the understanding of information and the ability to use that understanding to produce results. Tomorrow's job titles may sound the same as they did in

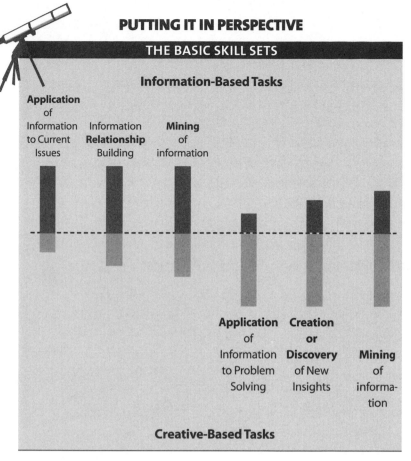

PUTTING IT IN PERSPECTIVE

THE BASIC SKILL SETS

Information-Based Tasks

Application of Information to Current Issues

Information **Relationship** Building

Mining of information

Application of Information to Problem Solving

Creation or Discovery of New Insights

Mining of information

Creative-Based Tasks

You must develop background in both information-based and creative-based skills. Your coursework should include classes that best develop this balance of creative and information analysis skill sets.

the past, but the actual responsibilities will be vastly different from what they were before the Information Age began.

When reviewing potential colleges, ask about the outcomes you can expect in your major rather than a list of prerequisites and courses that you will be taking. These outcomes should prepare you for the work world of the future. In the future, the value others place on your job market skills will depend on your ability to bring understanding to the market. The relatively new phrase "information worker" has already become commonplace, and within the next few years, it will sound archaic. A more appropriate name for an information worker will be an "understanding worker." Career success will depend on your ability to understand and create relationships among sets or pieces of information, whether they are facts and figures, artistic expressions, creative insights, or interpretations and applications.

71. Attend a Very Good Public University

So you can't, or don't want to go to one of the top public universities. You can still attend a very good public institution and get most of the benefits of attending one of the top twenty public universities (Cost-Saving Strategy 87).

The real difference between the best public universities (top twenty) and the next tier of schools has a lot to do with factors that probably have little importance to most undergraduate

> **Stat-to-Know**
>
> The average annual tuition at these universities is $3,700 for in-state students.

students. The second-tier colleges are often put in a lower class because of the size of their research budget, number of faculty with international reputations, size of the library, accomplishments of alumni, and financial savings (endowment). Most of these items are of little importance for the average undergraduate student. Thus many of these rankings have almost no bearing on the value of the education you will receive.

THE WINNERS

VERY GOOD SECOND-TIER PUBLIC UNIVERSITIES

State	University
Alabama	Auburn University
Arizona	University of Arizona
California	University of California-Los Angeles
Connecticut	University of Connecticut
Delaware	University of Delaware
Florida	University of Florida
Georgia	University of Georgia
Illinois	University of Illinois-Chicago
Indiana	Purdue University-West Lafayette
Iowa	University of Iowa
Maine	University of Maine-Orono
Maryland	University of Maryland-College Park
Massachusetts	University of Massachusetts-Amherst
Michigan	Michigan State University
Missouri	University of Missouri-Columbia
Nebraska	University of Nebraska-Lincoln`
New Hampshire	University of New Hampshire
New Jersey	Rutgers University-New Brunswick
North Carolina	North Carolina State University-Raleigh
Ohio	Ohio State University-Columbus
South Carolina	Clemson University
Tennessee	University of Tennessee-Knoxville
Texas	Texas A & M-College Station
Virginia	College of William & Mary
Washington	Washington State University
Wisconsin	University of Wisconsin-Milwaukee

72. Avoid Party Schools

Party atmosphere should not be one of your critical criteria in selecting a college. Students who select a "party school" usually do so for one of three reasons:

1. The academics tend to be easy, leaving lots of time to party.

2. These colleges have large numbers of students who come to school to party, providing plenty of people to party with. They attract large numbers of similar students.

3. They are often located in regions known for recreational attractions like skiing, surfing, or mountaineering.

While student polls show that only a very small percentage of students feel that partying is an important objective of college, many select schools with this type of reputation. Many of these students come from fairly wealthy high school districts and follow a tradition from their home area of attending specific party colleges.

INSIDER'S ADVICE

COMMON OUTCOMES AT PARTY SCHOOLS

▶ Longer than average time to graduation

▶ Higher transfer rates

▶ Poor career preparation

▶ Lack of employer respect

▶ Low acceptance rate to graduate schools

▶ Weak networking opportunities

▶ Marginal grade performance

▶ Development of poor habits

▶ Expensive surrounding communities

▶ Low graduation rates

Students rarely select these types of programs with career considerations or cost management in mind.

You should consider a number of different goals when selecting a college, and having a good time should be in the mix. However, entertainment should not be at the top of the list. Many students learn too late that a good time depends more on a state of mind than a location. They can find fun at most colleges and universities, especially those located in metropolitan areas with lots of choices and amenities.

PROFILES

Lexi went to a college on the ocean. It was a school that drew ten to twenty students from her high school every year. She reported at her college graduation that she had developed no contacts or work experience while in school. When she returned to the Midwest to find work she was at point zero. She had developed no contacts and had no local internship experience.

---

73. Seek Out Regional Accreditation

Evaluating the quality of an institution of higher education can be difficult. But if you decide to transfer to another college, you will soon learn about accreditation. The most common and generally accepted standard for evaluating a college or

Stat-to-Know

There are now more post-secondary schools without regional accreditation than there are with it.

university is accreditation. Schools turn to many groups for accreditation, but regional accrediting bodies have the most credibility. These accrediting agencies break the United States into six regions. Accrediting agencies measure schools against certain criteria or standards. When a college becomes accredited, it qualifies for federal and state financial aid programs. Accredited schools provide you the best guarantee that credits earned at one institution will later transfer to another.

Schools accredited by groups other than the regional accrediting commissions may qualify for government financial aid, but many of these colleges will not be recognized by other colleges and universities when it comes to transferring college credits or enrolling in graduate school. This is especially true for students at for-profit (proprietary) schools who may later want to have credits accepted at a college or university. Before choosing a college, consider how its accreditation status will affect your potential transfer to other colleges or universities.

The regional accrediting agencies are the Middle States Association, North Central Association, Southern Association, New England Association, Western Association, and Northwest

---

PROFILES

Manny attended a proprietary school for a year and a half and earned a diploma. Two years later he enrolled at a local community college to work toward an associate's degree. He was shocked to learn that none of his previous course work would transfer in. He was told it was because the proprietary school he attended did not have regional accreditation.

Association. Look for them in the catalog of the college of your choice. They are the "gold seal" of approval. You can also contact the accrediting agencies directly to obtain a list of all accredited schools in their region.

74. Match Your Learning Style

Some of us learn best through what we hear, others by what we do. You may require individual attention and others want to learn on their own. Only you know what works best for you. Identify your learning style from past coursework and find a college that fits this approach. By visiting college classes and talking with enrolled students, you get an idea of the teaching styles. Every college, department, and major will have different approaches to meeting learning styles. There are many different approaches to teaching. Here are a few of the most obvious:

- **Structured vs. Spontaneous Planning** – *Is the program structured or flexible enough to meet individual needs and interests?*

- **Active vs. Passive** – *Does the coursework require discussion, or is it based mostly on straight lecture?*

- **Comprehensive vs. Mastery** – *Is the coursework seen as a single unit or delivered in a step-by-step fashion?*

- **Independent vs. Interactive**– *Is group work required or is independent study the norm?*

- **Micro vs. Macro** – *Does the curriculum take a shotgun approach to topics or focus tightly on subjects?*

PROFILES

Juan started college at a large university that had large lecture classes, some with as many as 500 students. He was pleased to learn that after each lecture, he met in a small group with a teaching assistant. In these seminar groups, he found discussion and individual attention. He knew from high school that these were important learning methods for him.

75. Investigate Support Services

Make sure you will get the type of support that you need to be successful. Support services consist of a comprehensive group of activities designed to support your academic work and assist you with personal issues. These services are usually found in resource cen-

CHECKLIST

THE TYPES OF SPECIAL SERVICES THAT SHOULD BE AVAILABLE TO YOU

▶ Career planning
▶ Personal counseling
▶ Academic advising
▶ Tutoring
▶ Support for special needs students
▶ Research skills development
▶ Remediation programs
▶ Test review programs
▶ Safety counseling
▶ Academic advising

▶ Job search skills development
▶ Testing
▶ ESL support programs
▶ Study skills development
▶ Conflict resolution mediation
▶ Interest assessment
▶ Learning style analysis
▶ Foreign student programs

ters with titles like Support Services, Student Services, Counseling, Advising, etc. When used effectively, these centers can dramatically improve the quality of education you receive.

76. Avoid Education Scams

Just because a college promotes a program, doesn't make it good. In their effort to cut operating costs and attract more students, colleges have come up with a number of creative ways to reduce expenses while still increasing your tuition. Most of these questionable practices have you pay full tuition even when little service is delivered. The programs include such things as independent study, credit for little or no coursework, and credit for life experience. These practices are not necessarily negative and are okay as a component of a solid education. But when a college tries to build your education in large part with these tools, you should be

CHECKLIST
COLLEGE PRACTICES THAT MAY BE QUESTIONABLE

▶ **Courses taught by Teaching Assistants:** Teaching assistants often don't plan to become teachers and have little training in teaching. The quality of education they deliver can be weak.

▶ **Credit for life experiences:** A way for colleges to give you credit without completing substantial course work and still charge you.

▶ **Portfolio assessment for college credit:** Can be a really subjective tool used to give students credit for previous skill development.

▶ **Independent Study:** Allows colleges to charge a student for an education that the student is primarily providing for themselves.

▶ **Credit for Work Experiences:** Allows a student to pay tuition to receive credit for their paid employment and interacting with their regular supervisor.

suspicious of the overall quality of the program. Some colleges use such questionable practices in order to benefit the institution rather than the student. No more than 20 percent of your total credits earned should come from these types of programs.

PROFILES

Juanita was enrolled in a degree-completion program that allowed her to take the equivalent of her last two years of college through a special adult degree program over a fifteen-month period. She attended class one night a week, and her program revolved around a paper she wrote about her prior skill development. The paper was broken into subject areas and completed in sections. She used the program to earn a bachelor's degree in operations management. Fifteen months after starting, Juanita had her degree, along with serious doubts about the quality of education she received. She also had questions of how well it prepared her for her current employer's expectations and her future career development.

77. Be Cautious of Distance Learning

Key Forecast

In the next five years, less than 3% of all degrees awarded will be earned entirely through distance learning.

No method of delivering education has received as much hype and attention as distance learning. Distance learning really refers to a number of different approaches for connecting students and faculty from remote locations. The name is used to describe video studios in which a course is broadcast to remote locations. At these sites, students can see and hear the instructor, and the instructor can hear and see the students. A more common form of distance learning involves a student at a remote computer terminal interacting with faculty and other students as they complete college-level coursework. These computer-based education programs take two different basic approaches.

The first approach requires the student to log-on in real time to a specific course. The student is locked into a schedule at a specific day and time each week. Other students and the instructor are also online. The instructor and students can interact, at least on a limited basis. The second method of computer delivery has a student interact with software (courseware) on the student's own schedule. Students work at their own pace and utilize "chat rooms" to make contact with other students and their instructor. Other methods include courses designed around courseware on software disks or videos mailed to a student. Many of these distance-learning options provide students with other technology-based services (Cost-Saving Strategy 79) such as online libraries, financial aid, course planning, etc.

Because colleges don't have to make investments in physical infrastructure and student services for these distance-learning programs, they usually charge a lower tuition rate than the average for comparable college programs. However, while about 80 percent of colleges offer distance-learning courses, the number of full-degree options remains limited. Many full-degree programs are being added by consortiums (groups of colleges or even an entire state) and by for-profit colleges being established by traditional colleges as a subsidiary operation.

While about 1.6 million college students will take a distance-learning course this year, very few of these students are full-time, on-line students. Most of the participants in these courses don't work toward a degree. Even among those in degree programs, the completion rate has been very low, far below the national average of students working toward traditionally delivered degrees.

Distance learning is a solution to students' concern for convenience, but it is rarely the best solution when traditional alternatives are available. In many ways, distance learning has raised more concerns than it has answered. Educators, accrediting agencies, and government agencies are all concerned with the quality control of such programs and the low completion rate of students enrolled in them. However, for the individual that is unable to conveniently get to a college, distance learning offers a realistic alternative.

INSIDER'S ADVICE

WHAT TO LOOK FOR IN A DISTANCE-LEARNING PROGRAM

▶ Accreditation by a regional accrediting agency (Cost-Saving Strategy 73)

▶ A record of success with other distance students

▶ Courseware using full video presentations

▶ Regular and mandatory contact with instructor and classmates

▶ On-line library access

▶ A tuition rate below the institution's regular rate

▶ Self-paced course work

▶ Frequent tests and feedback

▶ A sound advisory program

▶ Clearly defined curriculum outcomes

78. Demand a Technology-Based Library

The primary purpose of a college library is to provide access to information and facilitate the sharing of information among all members of the academic community—faculty, staff, students, and alumni. This service must provide for a wide variety of information needs and also offer the tools that help people use the information. While many people felt that the Internet would make libraries obsolete, the opposite is true. The traditional search engines used by individuals in their home Internet work can directly access less than 1 percent of what exists on the Web. When you combine that with the fact that most users are fairly ineffective researchers, you can see why they end up finding even less information than that 1 percent of available material. A strong library can assist you in making use of other information sources and provides databases that are available to subscribers only.

A good library also must provide for other media such as audiovisual systems, digital web bands, DVD players, digital cameras, scanners, and virtual reality devices. Traditional low-tech services represent some of the most important services delivered by a college library. The nature of these services has changed over time. Today's low-tech services include staff assistance in the use of electronic offerings, assistance in research, help with database management, instruction in research skills, and the coordination of communications among various groups in the college.

A college library today is more than a building. It is an electronic campus that allows faculty, staff, and students access twenty-four-hours a day, seven days a week. All of these groups need access from remote locations and an accessible technology link between classroom and library resources. Students should have continuous connection to electronic library resources, including works reserved by faculty members for a specific class. Modern libraries should allow students to access, from remote locations, faculty-posted questions, and discussion items directly linked to commercial databases used for research and investigation.

79. Look for a Technology-Centered Education

The availability and use of technology on college campuses varies greatly from one school to the next. While every college claims to have all the latest technical innovations, you will find that many colleges lack fairly common technological services.

> **Stat-to-Know**
>
> Colleges report that at least 1/3 of their tuition increases are to pay for new technology—many have little to show for it.

Students should expect to use technology services in classrooms as well as for administrative functions, research tools, communications, and coursework management. Students and college administrators don't always agree on what technology services are most important.

An ideal college will seamlessly integrate technology into every course, from liberal-arts offerings to computer studies. It will also allow you to use the computer in all facets of your education.

By visiting a course management web site, you should be able to review class assignments, discussions, help programs, required readings, research material, and review your grades. During class periods, your instructor should be tied to the Internet and use it as a teaching tool to support lectures. Classes should offer simulation activities and research tools.

CHECKLIST

TECHNOLOGY SERVICES THAT SHOULD BE AVAILABLE TO STUDENTS

▶ **Electronic Communications** – E-mail should be campuswide

▶ **Research Software Tools** –That can be used for statistical analysis

▶ **Faculty Contact** – Direct electronic links to faculty courseware

▶ **Hands-on Computer Training** – Basic software skills

▶ **Computer Equipment Availability** – From every campus location

▶ **Automated Administrative Functions** – As needed by students

▶ **Classroom Technology** – Internet connection with projection capabilities

▶ **Coursework Management Systems** – With outlines, readings, grades, etc.

▶ **Technology Health Services** – On-line health services, pharmacy, and counseling

Administrative services might include the ability for you to register, change, and verify registration electronically. At some colleges it will allow you to check grades, transcripts, billing information, and financial aid data. In short, it can provide a doorway to all of your administrative service needs.

80. Find a Campus Convenient to Your Lifestyle

Today's students have a list of commitments that is much longer than students had in the past. Few schools have responded totally to this lifestyle change. Colleges should offer you convenience and fit in with all of your other commitments rather than making you decide between having a life and going to college. The old model of a new high school graduate going off to live at college now represents fewer than 20 percent of college students. Students often have children, jobs, homes, hobbies, and churches to balance with their college life.

Key Forecast

By 2010, more students will attend college off the main campus then on it.

The majority of students want a college that offers a location near their home or work, with convenient and safe parking or transportation. The financial aid department, bookstore, and advising offices should keep reasonable hours so you can use them when you need them, not on their schedule. Course offering schedules should be flexible and sensitive to your needs.

81. Design Your Own Curriculum

Make sure that your academic program fits your needs. While colleges develop curriculum plans with concern for a well-balanced educational experience, some have not changed much for several decades. While these programs can deliver a quality education and a degree, their content may not relate to today's world. Colleges maintain outdated curriculum in part because they find it difficult to get everyone to agree on what changes to make. Most colleges have tenured faculty in specialized areas of study, whom they quite simply need to utilize. So, even if a college determines that it needs a change in curriculum, it may not change simply because the college needs students enrolled in departments where it has lifetime commitments to faculty.

Another reason to critically look at a college's curriculum model is that institutions often design their programs for the average student attending their college. That means that most programs fit almost no one, but come close to fitting a large number of students. As a student, you should carefully design a curriculum that best meets your needs. You have the right in most cases to design your own curriculum plan, as long as you satisfy the requirements to earn a degree. You should build your course of study around your specific education and career goals, not the institution's preconceived idea of what you need (Cost-Saving Strategy 69). The selection of the right college minor can make the difference in

INSIDER'S ADVICE

MINORS THAT ARE ATTRACTIVE TO EMPLOYERS

- ▶ Accounting
- ▶ Adult Education
- ▶ Business Writing
- ▶ Communications
- ▶ Computer Applications
- ▶ Computer Programming
- ▶ Computer Science
- ▶ Economics
- ▶ Finance
- ▶ Foreign Language
- ▶ Graphic Arts
- ▶ Graphic Representation
- ▶ Human Resource Management

- ▶ Information Systems
- ▶ International Business
- ▶ Investment Management
- ▶ Management
- ▶ Marketing
- ▶ Network Management
- ▶ Project Management
- ▶ Quantitative Analysis
- ▶ Sales Management
- ▶ Statistics
- ▶ Technical Writing
- ▶ Telecommunications
- ▶ Web Commerce
- ▶ Web Design

landing the job you want. A college minor—usually four to six courses in a specific field—is very important to employers. It suggests versatility on your part if you have a "second" skill.

82. Select Practitioner-Based Education

Practitioner-based education finds its roots in the tradition of students working with masters of specialized subjects. Many fields lend themselves to this type of applied education, which in its basic form, utilizes practicing professionals as instructors. These professionals may be taking time out from their professional work or teaching part time while still working in their field.

Practitioners bring a great resource to the classroom. They share with students real-world, problem-solving experiences and pro-

INSIDER'S ADVICE

QUALITIES TO LOOK FOR IN A PRACTITIONER-BASED EDUCATION

▶ Strong core of full-time faculty

▶ One-half of courses delivered by practicing professionals (Practitioners)

▶ Few to no courses taught by teaching assistants

▶ Career and liberal arts and sciences courses integrated throughout the curriculum

▶ Credit earned from professional experiences such as internships

▶ Opportunity for the full-time worker to attend school full-time

▶ Individual attention and guidance

▶ Small class size

▶ Technology-assisted instruction

vide outstanding role models for students considering various career options. Most educators agree that students should learn in a context-sensitive environment, which means that the material covered in a course uses practical, realistic examples and problems that relate to the student's major.

Sound practitioner education also incorporates internships and externships. It brings local cultural institutions into the school and provides mentoring and professional guidance.

83. Transfer in the Off-Quarter for Easier Admission

Review the admissions requirements for transfer students and the number of seats made available for them each year. Colleges use a different set of admission criteria when evaluating transfer students. Some senior institutions welcome transfers, but others strictly limit the number of transfers accepted. Consider starting the senior institution at a time other than the fall semester. Many colleges keep more spots available for transfer students in the spring or winter terms after fall starts drop out. You will have a better chance of getting into your school of choice during these terms.

84. Go to the Head of the Class

So you can't gain acceptance to one of the top private or public universities in the country, and you wonder if you should try to get into one of the second-tier institutions? Second-tier colleges are those that fall just below the top colleges or universities in the national rankings found in a number of magazine surveys. Despite what the school's marketing departments might tell you, little evidence supports the position that second-tier schools offer any significant extra value or success potential over third-tier or fourth-tier colleges.

Unless you plan to attend one of the top forty colleges, you should evaluate your school choice based on the best fit for you. A weaker student at a second-tier school has no edge over a top student at a lower-ranked college. You might actually be better off being one of the top students at a college rather than being an average student at a higher ranked institution. Once they start searching below the top forty colleges, employers recruiting new graduates will look more closely at your performance in school than on the reputation of the institution you attended.

INSIDER'S ADVICE

EVALUATING WHICH LEVEL OF COLLEGE TO ATTEND.

▶ Your test scores should put you in the top half of the entering classes

▶ Your strengths should be in a strong unit of the institution

▶ The graduation rate in your chosen field should be at or above the institutions average rate

▶ Your choice of major should be one of the strongest departments of the college

PROFILES

Louise was intent on getting into "the best" college that she could. She felt that her test scores did not reflect her real ability and that by working hard she could make up for any deficiencies she might have. She was accepted into one of her top choices, a school where her test scores and high school rank put her in the bottom half of the entering class. She graduated five years later with a degree in communications. She began her job search after earning a grade point average just below a B and a rank just below the midpoint of her class. She had received no honors in school and found little time to develop any job-related skills or volunteer activities. Louise ended up accepting a position outside her area of study, at a lower salary than she had hoped.

Hector's test scores in high school weren't quite good enough to get him into an elite university. But he pretty much had his choice of other quality colleges and universities. He selected what most people consider the second-best public four-year university in his home state. His entering test scores put him in the top half of the entering class. He enrolled in the honors curriculum and received a great deal of individual advising and mentoring in the formal class sessions. Hector finished in four years after turning an internship into a part-time job during his junior year. At graduation, he ranked in the top 10 percent of his class with a high B average and turned his communications degree into an outstanding full-time position at the company where he had served as an intern.

85. Slide in the Back Door

There is more than one way to get into a college. If you intend to apply to a college with a strong reputation but don't have the grades and/or test scores to get into one of these top schools through normal channels, you might want to slide in the back door.

Key Forecast

Many top universities will be adding "back door" programs as new revenue sources.

A number of universities with great academic reputations offer little-known programs that give students the opportunity to attend the school through a separate division (i.e., university college, continuing studies, adult studies). These alternative tracks have less-stringent admissions requirements and charge a lower tuition rate. Such programs can save you up to 50 percent on tuition costs and get you a lot more "college reputation" than you ever thought would be possible.

Many colleges provide these "back door" programs. You need to hunt through a school's catalog to discover them. Some colleges require applicants to these programs to be twenty-one years of age with some work experience.

THE WINNERS

COLLEGES AND UNIVERSITIES WITH SPECIAL ADMISSION PROGRAMS

State	*College / University*
Alabama	University of Alabama
Colorado	Colorado State University
Connecticut	University of Connecticut
District of Columbia	American University
	Catholic University of America
	Howard University
	Georgetown University

State	College / University
Florida	University of Miami
Illinois	Loyola University-Chicago
	Northwestern University
Indiana	Indiana University
Iowa	University of Iowa
Louisiana	Tulane University
Massachusetts	Boston College
	Boston University
	Harvard University
Michigan	Wayne State University
Missouri	Washington University
New York	Fordham University
	New York University
Ohio	Bowling Green State
	Ohio State University
	University of Akron
	University of Cincinnati
Pennsylvania	University of Pittsburgh
Virginia	Old Dominion
	University of Virginia
	Virginia Commonwealth University
Washington	Washington State University
Wisconsin	Marquette University

> **PROFILES**
>
> Ada was thirty-eight when she decided to finish her bachelor of arts degree. As a working mother she knew she would have a tough time earning a degree. Although she had attended a number of different colleges, she only had 27 semester hours of college credit. As a young woman, she had always wanted to attend a top twenty university. She knew she would not come close to the applicant profile needed for regular admission. After some study, she discovered she could attend her university of choice by enrolling in the evening continuing studies division as an adult, continuing student.

86. Earn Admission to One of the Most Prestigious Private Universities

If you can get into one of the top twenty private universities, you should consider the tuition a good investment, it is probably underpriced in spite of all of the complaints you hear about high costs.

For the most part, a college's reputation has little impact on future career advancement. But the top prestigious schools are an exception to the rule. "Prestige" can have different meanings, but educators agree on which are the top schools. All of these universities have outstanding reputations with employers, a high rate of acceptance to graduate and professional schools, and international alumni networks very interested in helping graduates. These schools are on the top of the recruitment lists at the most sought-after organizations.

The top twenty-three enroll a large percentage of the very best students in the country. This creates a very competitive environment both for students trying to get in and for students once admitted. This competition has not gone unnoticed by companies and organizations seeking to hire new college graduates. Most of the top firms focus a great deal of their attention on the graduates from these top twenty-three institutions because they know that only the best students can gain admission to such schools. In recent years, a little of this recruiting edge has moderated, as smaller firms do more of the new hiring. However, most of them cannot afford the high salaries demanded by graduates of top schools. There is a clear advantage for graduates of these top twenty-three universities.

But don't panic if you can't meet the stiff admissions criteria of these institutions. They are not the only paths to success. Success stories abound of individuals who went to less prestigious schools or who didn't attend college at all, and became multimillionaires.

THE WINNERS

PRESTIGIOUS PRIVATE UNIVERSITIES

State	University
California	California Institute of Technology
	Stanford University
	University of Southern California
Connecticut	Yale University
District of Columbia	Georgetown University
Georgia	Emory University
Illinois	Northwestern University
	University of Chicago
Indiana	University of Notre Dame

(Continued)

PRESTIGIOUS PRIVATE UNIVERSITIES (Continued)	
State	*University*
Maryland	Johns Hopkins University
Massachusetts	Harvard University
	Massachusetts Institute of Technology
New Hampshire	Dartmouth University
New Jersey	Princeton University
New York	Columbia University
	Cornell University
North Carolina	Duke University
	Wake Forest University
Pennsylvania	Carnegie Mellon University
	University of Pennsylvania
Rhode Island	Brown University
Tennessee	Vanderbilt University
Texas	Rice University

These institutions enjoy the reputation they do in part because of their rigorous admissions requirements. A typical year for these colleges would see them accepting fewer than 10 percent of those who apply. Less than 1 percent of college students attend a prestigious private university.

87. Consider the Top Public Universities

If you can't get into or pay for the most prestigious private schools, you should consider the top publics. These public universities offer a high-quality education at tremendous tuition savings over the privates. They typically don't boast the alumni network of the top privates, their students often take a lot of classes taught by teaching assistants, and the large student bodies make the education seem less personalized. Yet many of them deliver an outstanding education and command the same type of respect accorded to the top private universities, especially in technical fields.

THE WINNERS

TOP PUBLIC UNIVERSITIES

State	University
California	University of California-Berkeley
Georgia	Georgia Institute of Technology
Illinois	University of Illinois-Urbana-Champaign
Michigan	University of Michigan-Ann Arbor
Minnesota	University of Minnesota
New York	SUNY
North Carolina	University of North Carolina-Chapel Hill
Pennsylvania	Pennsylvania State-University Park
Texas	University of Texas-Austin
Virginia	University of Virginia
Washington	University of Washington
Wisconsin	University of Wisconsin-Madison

Most of these top publics are huge universities. They attract the lion share of America's strongest students. More of the top students are turning to the publics for the great value to cost ratio they deliver. You can counterbalance the size of these institutions by strategically planning and controlling your education.

INSIDER'S ADVICE

HOW TO SUCCEED AT A LARGE UNIVERSITY

▶ Quickly establish a relationship with a mentor

▶ Join a group or club to meet people

▶ Put extra effort into large lecture classes

▶ Attend all of your classes

▶ Have written record of an approved course plan

▶ Find ways around "flunk-out" courses

▶ Form a strong bond to your major field faculty

▶ Meet and make friends with graduate students in your department

▶ Learn the campus right away

▶ Bring your own computer technology

▶ Establish electronic communication links to all of your faculty

88. Study Abroad

Enhance your education by seeing the world. The rapidly expanding world economy has led modern business leaders to seek employees who understand a second language and different cultures. Many students polish these skills through one or two semesters of study in a foreign country. While almost every college will allow you to study abroad, not all schools do a good job of making these programs a reasonable option. Look for colleges that have developed policies and practices that allow you to study abroad without losing any time toward graduation. The number of students studying abroad has not increased in recent years even as college enrollments have grown. Schools do not routinely provide prospective students with enough information about foreign-study programs. When looking at prospective study-abroad programs, be sure that the institution has a large number of students that have annually studied abroad and a clear record of these students graduating in a timely fashion. The tuition rate for study abroad should be similar to the main campus rate and college-sponsored housing should be available.

WINNERS

COLLEGES WITH OUTSTANDING STUDY ABROAD PROGRAMS

State	University
Arizona	University of Arizona
Colorado	University of Colorado-Boulder
Illinois	University of Illinois-Urbana-Champaign
Indiana	University of Notre Dame
Massachusetts	Boston College
Michigan	Michigan State University
Minnesota	St. Olaf College
New Hampshire	Dartmouth College
New York	Colgate University
North Carolina	University of North Carolina-Chapel Hill
Ohio	Miami University-Oxford
Pennsylvania	University of Pennsylvania
Texas	University of Texas-Austin
Utah	Brigham Young University
Virginia	George Mason University
Wisconsin	University of Wisconsin-Madison

PROFILES

Peter attended the state university near where he had grown up. He started at age eighteen and wanted to graduate in four years. Peter had never been out of the Midwest. When given a choice to spend his junior year of college studying in Italy, he jumped at it. It was a perfect experience for anyone in his major of art history. It brought all of his textbooks to life and allowed him a culturally broadening experience that would serve him for life.

89. Review the College Mission

Make sure you know what a college stands for. Every college has a mission or purpose statement, which can give you insight into what the school values. As an undergraduate, you should look for a mission focused on teaching undergraduates. If the emphasis is on research, running a hospital, expensive graduate programs, or building a religious experience, you may want to think twice about this college choice. This is especially true of private universities that may be funding these endeavors with resources they should be using to educate you.

Public universities typically receive special funding for each unit (graduate school, research center, hospital) from specially funded state, federal, and local agencies. Private schools on the other hand, have the freedom to move dollars around to cover their own priorities.

Students often report that they selected an undergraduate college because it also had a medical, dental, law, or other profes-

INSIDER'S ADVICE

WHAT TO LOOK FOR IN A MISSION STATEMENT.

▶ The primary focus on teaching

▶ A commitment to undergraduate education

▶ A list of expected undergraduate outcomes

▶ Secondary status given to research and community service programs

▶ Concern for total individual well-being

▶ A commitment to the use of technology in the education process

sional school of interest to them. The truth is that unless you pursue a dual degree program (Cost-Saving Strategy 18), you will probably gain no edge in the admission process for professional schools simply because you attended the same college as an undergraduate. In some cases, it may actually hurt your chances of acceptance to the professional school, as professional programs like to get a diverse population representing a large number of colleges and universities.

CHAPTER 9

Get Better Long-Term Return on Your Investment with Career Development

A ll of the strategies in this section are designed to help you build the financial return you will receive from your investment in college. The largest financial return usually comes from your career development. It is a measure of lifetime earnings. A good education will prepare you for both today's and tomorrow's job market.

90. Attend School in a City

Location isn't everything but it is extremely important. College location is much more critical than many people realize. Thirty years ago, students often selected colleges based on how comfortable they felt with the town or city size and a generalized impression of the people who lived there. Today's student more critically evaluates a college location based on what the town or city contributes to the quality of education. This is one of the reasons that going to school in a large city has become such a popular choice. In some ways, not much has changed from the days when we were predominately an agricultural country and agriculture was at the center of learning. Many of our great universities were established around schools of agriculture. They were located in rural areas. Today, we live in a technology-based world, and areas that lead the nation in information technology, telecommunications, health-care technology, and service industries make the most ideal settings for colleges or universities. These are usually big cities.

The best opportunities come in cities that possess a diverse industry base with strong growth in jobs and new businesses. Attending a college in the midst of cornfields may seem peaceful and contemplative, but such a location can hurt students who want to focus on their future career while still in college. Colleges in metro areas offer career, cultural, and entertainment experiences not available elsewhere.

Cities like Chicago, Los Angeles, Boston, New York, and Washington D.C. offer extensive opportunities for volunteering, internships, externships, part-time employment, and full-time employment. They also provide classroom enrichment opportunities when working practitioners serve as guest lecturers or teach courses. In fields where technology changes on eight- to twelve-month life cycles, it is critical that you learn from practitioner instructors who are immersed in these technologies on a daily basis.

Outside of the classroom, large metropolitan areas offer great opportunities for mentoring. Mentors can give you much-needed direction in curriculum planning and help in selecting a major. Mentoring can also lead to networking opportunities for future part-time and full-time employment. Professional organizations locate their headquarters and schedule meetings and conferences in large cities. Students involved in these activities get a special admission rate and access to leaders in their field.

Your coursework represents only a fraction of your college experience, and you will find more opportunities to enhance your practical experiences in major metropolitan locations. With the large and growing industry base in these areas you can expect salaries for part-time work and internships to be 15 to 20 percent higher than average.

THE WINNERS

GOOD CITY COLLEGES

City	University
Atlanta	The Atlanta College of Art
	Emory University
	Georgia Institute of Technology
	Georgia State University
	Morehouse College
Boston	Boston University
	Emerson College
	Massachusetts College of Art
	Northeastern University
	University of Massachusetts-Boston
	Wentworth Institute of Technology
Chicago	Columbia College
	DePaul University
	Illinois Institute of Technology
	Loyola University-Chicago
	Northeastern Illinois University
	Robert Morris College
	Roosevelt University
	School of the Art Institute of Chicago
	University of Chicago
	University of Illinois-Chicago

(Continued)

GOOD CITY COLLEGES (Continued)

City	University
Denver	Metropolitan State College of Denver
	University of Colorado-Denver
	University of Denver
Los Angeles	Loyola Marymount University
	Occidental College
	University of California-Los Angeles
	University of Southern California
New York City	Audrey Cohen College
	Barnard College
	CUNY
	Columbia University
	Fordham University
	New York University
	Pace University
San Francisco	Golden Gate University
	San Francisco State University
	University of San Francisco
Washington, D.C.	American University
	Catholic University of America
	George Washington University
	Georgetown University
	Howard University
	University of the District of Columbia

PROFILES

Jane always wanted to attend a large university in a "college town" setting. In her junior year of college she wanted and needed to work. She decided it would be great to find work related to her major—marketing. After searching for three months she ended up settling for a job in a campus cafeteria. There were just no jobs available in this small town and any job that did open had hundreds of potential candidates.

Her sister Emily who attended a college in the heart of Chicago had two part-time job offers related to her major of accounting. She landed the jobs through one of her instructors who taught part-time and worked for a large CPA firm. After taking her pick, she did an eighteen-month internship and was offered a full-time job with the firm after graduation.

91. Compare Possible Major Choices

Today's new college graduates enter an uncertain job market, with labor shortages in some fields amidst reports of layoffs in others. This makes your career field selection more critical than ever. In some areas of the country and in particular fields, the wrong major choice can be very costly. To analyze major choices, you need to consider the number of offers received, the quality of initial job responsibilities, and starting salaries offered to recent graduates of this field. For example, engineers had average starting annual salaries of over $50,000 in 2001, while graduates entering social science-related jobs earned average annual salaries of under $30,000. Over the course of a working lifetime, this translates into the engineering graduate making twice the total earnings of the social science graduate.

Before you choose a major, answer the following checklist questions. They will help you identify what you expect out of your college education. Is college a rite of passage or are you expecting big returns on your investment of time and money?

CHECKLIST

CHECKLIST

JOB POTENTIAL TODAY
Will graduates of this major find jobs?

CAREER POTENTIAL TOMORROW
How will study in this field impact my long-term career opportunities?

INTENSITY OF STUDY REQUIRED
How hard is the coursework in this field?

ACHIEVEMENTS AND PRIOR ACADEMIC PREPARATION
Do I have the aptitude for this field of study?

CAREER EXPECTATIONS
Does this major match my career expectations?

ADMISSIONS REQUIREMENTS
How likely am I to get into a good program in this field?

LIFESTYLE
How will this major impact my life commitments?

PERSONAL INTERESTS
Do my interests match the required coursework?

Answering these questions should help you narrow your choice from the long list of available majors. If nothing else, it should at least point to families of related majors that best fit your personal profile.

92. Meet Employers' Needs

If you wish to prepare for the work world, you need to determine the type of education employers want you to have. In an earlier section, we discussed the types of colleges employers look to first when hiring new college graduates. In this section we look at the specific types of programs employers seek.

A recent poll of 800 chief executive officers from a wide variety of organization sizes in a large metropolitan setting showed a clear preference for hiring college graduates with applied degrees.

Stat to Know

93% of CEOs report they look first for applied degree holders when making new hires.

PUTTING IT IN PERSPECTIVE

PERCENT OF SURVEYED CEOs RESPONDING THIS IS AN IMPORTANT TRAIT OF NEW HIRES	
Applied Degree	93%
Internship/Externship	75%
Strong Grades	73%
Technical Skills	70%
Communication Skills	67%
Diverse Student Experience	56%
Ability to Work with Others	53%
Reputation of College	41%

0%   20%   40%   60%   80%   100%

Different types of organizations have different needs, but most want graduates with applied degrees. The size of hiring firms impacts their needs. Most new jobs are created by companies with fewer than 100 employees. These firms need employees who can contribute to end results from day one. They need people with multiple skill sets that don't require long, formal training programs. What training that does occur is usually on the firing line when the results count.

INSIDER'S ADVICE

HOTTEST CAREER FIELDS FOR THE NEXT DECADE

▶ Adult Education

▶ Architectural Design

▶ Athletic Podiatry

▶ Aviation Security

▶ Bioengineering

▶ Biomechanics

▶ Biomedical Engineering

▶ Biotechnology

▶ Career Counseling

▶ Cellular System Programming

▶ Chemical Engineering

▶ City Planning

▶ Civil Engineering

▶ Construction Engineering

▶ Cosmetic Dentistry

▶ Culinary Arts

▶ Dental Hygiene

▶ Electronic Auditing

▶ Electronic Communication Systems

▶ Electronic Engineering

▶ Electronic Entertainment

▶ Electronic Monitoring Systems

▶ Electronic Security Systems

▶ Electronics

▶ Elementary Education

▶ Environment Systems Engineering

- ▶ Fitness Specialist
- ▶ Forensic Medicine
- ▶ Geriatric Counseling
- ▶ Geriatric Medicine
- ▶ Geriatric Rehab
- ▶ Graphic Representation
- ▶ Hospitality Management
- ▶ Internet Marketing
- ▶ Medical Assisting
- ▶ Medical Profiling
- ▶ Medical System Technology
- ▶ Network Management
- ▶ Network Security
- ▶ Nursing
- ▶ Occupational Therapy
- ▶ Personal Enrichment Counseling
- ▶ Personal Environment
- ▶ Personal Financial Management
- ▶ Pharmacology
- ▶ Physical Therapy
- ▶ Recreation Management
- ▶ Rehab Chiropractics
- ▶ Restaurant Management
- ▶ Retail Profiling
- ▶ Risk Management
- ▶ Secondary Education
- ▶ Security Analysis
- ▶ Security Management

(Continued)

HOTTEST CAREER FIELDS FOR THE NEXT DECADE (Continued)
▶ Special Education
▶ Sports Management
▶ Substance Engineering
▶ System Auditing
▶ Telecommunications
▶ Web Commerce
▶ Web Design
▶ Web System Management
▶ Wireless System Design

93. Build an Alumni Network

A good indicator of the job development potential of a college is the strength of its alumni network. You can measure alumni networking potential in a number of ways. The number of graduates is one indicator, but perhaps the best is alumni support of the college. If individuals are willing to give money and time to their alma matter, there is probably a strong bond with what that college is doing and with its current students.

THE WINNERS

COLLEGES WITH STRONG ALUMNI NETWORKS	
State	*University*
California	Stanford University
	University of California-Berkeley
	University of California-Los Angeles
	University of Southern California

State	University
Connecticut	Yale University
Illinois	Northwestern University
Indiana	DePauw University University of Notre Dame
Massachusetts	Harvard University Massachusetts Institute of Technology
Michigan	University of Michigan
Nebraska	University of Nebraska
New Hampshire	Dartmouth College
New Jersey	Princeton University
New York	Cornell University Columbia University
North Carolina	Duke University University of North Carolina-Chapel Hill
Pennsylvania	University of Pennsylvania

94. Gain Work Experience

Work experience may prove to be as valuable as classroom performance with many potential employers. Some colleges will actually give you credit for work experience that augments your classroom study. That kind of recognition from your school can make your résumé look stronger to potential employers and cut your total cost of tuition. Look for work that has a tie to your field of study, but try to relate everything you do at work to your major. Don't earn more than 20 percent of your total credit through credit for work programs.

95. Complete an Internship

Several hundred years ago, interns were called apprentices. Instead of just learning the basics of a craft, the apprentice would often devote ten, twenty, or even more years to working with a master artisan or artist. The apprentice would forever be known as the student of the master unless he, too, created an outstanding work that elevated him to the level of master.

This educational concept has stayed with us for generations. In fields such as teaching, nursing, and medicine, classroom work is combined with "field experience" under the tutelage of practicing experts. The combination of strong classroom academics and hands-on experience from internships form the basis for an outstanding college experience. Make sure your choice of college curriculum offers the opportunity for an internship.

A college education should involve three distinct levels of instruction. There should be classroom instruction using the latest technology and real world problem-solving applications. There should be a strong core of foundation courses that relate to world issues. Lastly, you should be given the opportunity to do internships.

As an intern, you gain the opportunity to work with today's masters. While you will not spend ten or twenty years as an intern, the experience will enrich your education. Some internships, often known as "externships," earn you course credit. Other internships may fall under the category of cooperative education, in which you take a job related to your field of study. While some internships pay a salary, many do not. They do however provide a way of acquiring work experience and a chance to experience the world of work in your chosen field.

Not all internships are the same quality. Talk to students who have taken an internship at the site you are considering.

INSIDER'S ADVICE

QUALITY INTERNSHIP PLANNING

What to Look For	What to Avoid
▶ Work in your major field	▶ Office flunky assignments
▶ An opportunity to do a variety of job assignments	▶ Work for more than one firm at a time
▶ Work with senior staff members	▶ Combining an internship with another job
▶ An evaluation plan with specific outcomes	▶ Reporting to a number of people
	▶ No specified schedule

PROFILES

Reena's internship was during her junior year of college. She worked as an aide to the creative director of an advertising agency. She was given her own projects to work on, and was allowed to participate in staff planning meetings and client visits. She loved the field, her boss, and the scope of the work she was involved with. The experience cemented her interest in the career field of advertising. She formed what she hoped would be a lifetime relationship with her mentor.

96. Look for a Diverse Student Body

Avoid schools that have a homogeneous study body of any type, whether it's all female, all Catholic, all older, all rich, or all anything. Employers look for individuals who come from heterogeneous educational experiences that more closely mirror the real world of work. Students who lack this exposure to diversity enter the job market at a disadvantage. It's critical that you know how to work cooperatively with different types of people. Different cultures express themselves, solve problems, react to situations, and lead in different ways. Students should strive to meet people with new ideas, who express unique attitudes and customs.

Employers look for this type of educational diversity when making hiring decisions. The following table shows you the types of diversity they value most.

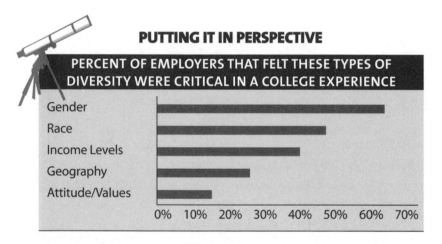

PUTTING IT IN PERSPECTIVE

PERCENT OF EMPLOYERS THAT FELT THESE TYPES OF DIVERSITY WERE CRITICAL IN A COLLEGE EXPERIENCE

Gender
Race
Income Levels
Geography
Attitude/Values

0% 10% 20% 30% 40% 50% 60% 70%

THE WINNERS

COLLEGES WITH DIVERSE STUDENT BODIES

State	University
Alabama	Troy State University-Montgomery
California	California State University-Long Beach
	San Jose State University
	University of San Francisco
	University of Southern California

State	University
Connecticut	University of Bridgeport
Florida	Barry University University of Miami
Georgia	Wesleyan College
Hawaii	Chaminade University of Honolulu Hawaii Pacific University
Illinois	Northeastern Illinois University University of Illinois-Chicago Robert Morris College
Indiana	Calumet College of St. Joseph Indiana University Northwest
Maryland	Columbia Union College
Massachusetts	Massachusetts Institute of Technology
Missouri	Lincoln University
New Jersey	New Jersey Institute of Technology Rutgers University-Newark St. Peter's College New Jersey City University
New York	College of Mount St. Vincent CUNY-Baruch College CUNY-City College CUNY-Hunter College
North Carolina	University of North Carolina-Pembroke
Texas	University of Houston University of Houston-Downtown
Virginia	Marymount University

97. Select a Major Based on Your Career Plans

Even if your plan is for continued study beyond the bachelor's degree, in a professional or graduate school program, you should earn your bachelor's degree in a career field, both as fail-safe protection and as an enhancement to your overall résumé even with a graduate degree. Eighty percent of job offers to college graduates will go to students studying in 20 percent of the majors. There are in essence two types of baccalaureate majors, those that lead directly to work at the bachelor's degree level and those that require advanced degrees to become job ready. The

Key Forecast

80% of job offers to college graduates will go to students who studied in 20% of the majors.

list of majors that lead to professional jobs in the field of study after earning a bachelor's degree are mostly applied degrees. All of the other majors usually require a graduate degree in order to find work in your field.

INSIDER'S ADVICE

MAJORS THAT LEAD DIRECTLY TO JOBS AT THE BACHELOR'S LEVEL	MAJORS THAT DO NOT LEAD DIRECTLY TO JOBS AT THE BACHELOR'S LEVEL
Accounting	American Studies
Actuarial Science	Anthropology
Advertising	Art
Aerospace Engineering	Art Design
Agriculture	Art History

(Continued)

MAJORS THAT LEAD DIRECTLY TO JOBS AT THE BACHELOR'S LEVEL	MAJORS THAT DO NOT LEAD DIRECTLY TO JOBS AT THE BACHELOR'S LEVEL
Architectural Engineering	Art (Studio)
Architecture	Arts & Letters–General
Business Administration	Arts & Letters–Honors
Chemical Engineering	Arts–Pre Professional Studies
Chemistry	Biochemistry
Civil Engineering	Biology
Commerce	Black Studies
Computer Aided Drafting	Botany
Computer Applications	Childcare Studies
Computer Networks	Classical Languages (Greek)
Computer Programming	Classical Languages (Latin)
Computer Science	Communication Arts
Computer Systems	Communications & Theatre
Consumer Economics	Dance
Criminal Justice & Administration	Earth Science
E-Commerce	English
Ecology	Fashion Design
Economics	Film Study
Education–Elementary	Fine Arts
Education–Secondary	General Science
Education–Specialist	General Studies
EEG Technology	Geography
Electrical & Computer Engineering	Government
Electrical Engineering	Health Sciences
Engineering Mechanics	History
	History & Philosophy of Science

(Continued)

MAJORS THAT LEAD DIRECTLY TO JOBS AT THE BACHELOR'S LEVEL	MAJORS THAT DO NOT LEAD DIRECTLY TO JOBS AT THE BACHELOR'S LEVEL
Engineering Science	Home Economics
Engineering Technology	Interdisciplinary Studies
Environment Control Technology	International Studies
Environmental Design	Journalism
Environmental Health Engineering	Literature
Finance	Medical Assisting
Fitness Technology	Medieval Studies
Geology	Microbiology
Graphic Art & Design	Military Science
Health Service Management	Music-Instrumental
Hospitality & Recreation	Music-Vocal
Hotel Management	Natural Science
Information Sciences	Philosophy
Institutional Administration	Physical Science
Interior Design	Political Science
International Business	Psychiatric Social Work
Management	Psychology
Marketing	Recreational Therapy
Material Science Engineering	Social Work
Math & Computer Science	Sociology
Mathematics	Sociology & Anthropology
Mechanical Engineering	Speech & Drama
Medical Assistant	Theology
Medical Records	Women's Studies
Metallurgical Engineering	Zoology

(Continued)

MAJORS THAT LEAD DIRECTLY TO JOBS AT THE BACHELOR'S LEVEL

Meteorology

Mining Engineering

Music Education

Naval Science

Nuclear Engineering

Nuclear Medicine Technology

Nursing

Occupational Therapy

Operations Research

Optometry

Paralegal Studies

Parks, Recreation, &
   Leisure Studies

Petroleum Engineering

Physical and Corrective
   Therapy Assisting

Physical Education

Physics

Radiology Technology

Respiratory Therapy

Securities & Financial Analysis

Social Work Assistance

Surgical Technology

Telecommunications

Travel & Tourism

Web Design

PROFILES

As an eighteen-year-old freshman, Katherine had no idea of what her major should be. She selected communications because she liked to be with people. With a degree in communications, Katherine could find no job in her area of specialization after she graduated. She did have two offers that had little to do with her six years of college study and that paid lower than average starting salaries. She decided to go to graduate school instead.

98. Number of Students Enrolled in Your Major

Key Forecast

In the next ten years, colleges will cut out 20% of their majors.

Be sure that a large percentage of the students enrolled at your college choice are studying in your field of study. No college is strong in all subject areas. Your ideal college should be strong in your major of interest. Remember that a college's general reputation is important for ranking the overall institution, but its reputation in your major is more important to you for career development purposes.

In some ways, you can determine a specific program's strength by the sheer size of a school or a department within a college. Most colleges will put more resources where they have more students. When forced to eliminate some program offerings, colleges will cut the smaller programs. Ask friends, relatives, and potential employers about a college's reputation in your major.

PROFILES

Taylor started college as a theater major. She attended a large university and liked the idea that the theater department was quite small—like family, in fact. Taylor felt she had the best of both worlds, a large school with a small department. The problem occurred when the Board of Trustees decided to close the Theater Department along with two others as a cost-cutting measure. They were all small departments with little clout. Taylor was forced to transfer or change majors. Both choices meant extra terms of study.

INSIDER'S ADVICE

WHAT MAKES A MAJOR SAFE FROM ELIMINATION AT COLLEGE?

▶ Large share of enrollment at the college

▶ One of the top reputation programs

▶ Faculty in the department that have prominent reputations

▶ Few similar programs at area colleges and universities

▶ Large number of endowed faculty positions

▶ Long list of prominent alumni

▶ Above average job placement prospects for graduates

▶ Buildings on campus dedicated to the major

99. Interdisciplinary Studies: Combined-Degree Programs

Buying two products for the price of one is usually a good deal. This is as true for college majors as it is for groceries. The majority of colleges offer some sort of combined degree in related subject areas. Combined degrees allow you to study a comprehensive set of advanced coursework from two or more fields. This is almost, but not quite, like earning two degrees. In a combined degree program you will earn one degree. With careful planning, you can improve in both the expertise you develop and in the employment value of your degree by developing credentials in two fields of study.

Some degree combinations present an opportunity for specialization not typically found at the undergraduate level. This is true when advanced coursework is allowed in both fields. Other colleges combine majors less for the association of coursework and more because they develop two related but separate skills.

Even if your college does not offer combined-degree programs, it may allow you to chose two majors. That option can accomplish just as much. Self-directed programs, such as with two majors, may take longer. In prepackaged combined-degree options, students can usually finish in the same time it takes to earn a single major degree.

INSIDER'S ADVICE

**THINGS TO DO WHEN CONSIDERING
COMBINED DEGREE PROGRAMS**

▶ Meet with faculty advisors from both departments regarding your program

▶ Find out how many students have graduated from the combined program option

▶ Have a clear idea of the benefits this program will give you

▶ Discuss with working professionals the value of these combined skills

▶ Be sure that you can graduate on your original timetable

CHECKLIST

COMMON COMBINED-DEGREE PROGRAMS

▶ Agriculture and Economics	▶ Computer Science and Math
▶ Anthropology and Sociology	▶ Computer Studies and Electrical Engineering
▶ Physics and Math	▶ Computer Science and Business
▶ Art History and Religion	▶ Education and Business
▶ Fine Art and Administration	▶ History and Political Science
▶ Business and Chemistry	▶ Music Performance and Literature
▶ Business and Humanities	▶ Philosophy and Physics
▶ Engineering and Management	

100. Evaluate Your Chances of Getting into Professional School

If you plan to continue your education in a "professional" school—a graduate program in medicine, law, business, dentistry, or veterinary medicine—you'll want to select a college with a good track record of getting its graduates into such professional programs. Many colleges offer special programs that prepare undergraduate students for admission and study in professional schools. Professional schools will tell you that it does not really matter where you earn your undergraduate degree. Don't believe them—it does matter.

Some colleges have specialized professional-prep majors that include coursework, mentoring, test preparation, advising, and help with the application process. Such programs have varying degrees of success in getting their students into graduate school.

INSIDER'S ADVICE

THINGS TO LOOK FOR IN A GOOD PROFESSIONAL-PREP PROGRAM

▶ Dedicated advisers for professional school candidates

▶ Specialized curriculum

▶ Joint programs with professional schools

▶ Professional school entrance test prep

▶ Record of success in getting graduates enrolled in graduate school

CHAPTER 10

100 Tips Comparison Matrix

Legend:
- **Above Average** = ●
- **Average** = ◐
- **Below Average** = ⊙

	Savings	Improve-ment to General Value	Avail-ability	Chance of Quali-fying	Impact on Long term Results
1. Attend a Community College	●	◐	●	●	●
2. Study Tuition Increase Patterns	◐	⊙	●	●	◐
3. Compare Tuition Rates	◐	⊙	●	●	◐
4. Consider States with Low In-state Tuition Rates	⊙	⊙	⊙	◐	◐
5. Study the Average Teaching Load	◐	◐	●	●	◐
6. Find a Guaranteed Tuition Rate	◐	⊙	⊙	◐	◐
7. Attend a Tuition-Free College	●	⊙	⊙	⊙	◐

Above Average ● Average ◐ Below Average ⊙	Savings	Improvement to General Value	Availability	Chance of Qualifying	Impact on Long term Results
8. Don't Pay Unnecessary Student Fees	◐	⊙	◐	●	◐
9. Commute to College	●	◐	●	●	◐
10. Don't Attend College Far from Home	◐	◐	●	●	◐
11. Build Equity in Your College Housing	●	⊙	⊙	●	◐
12. Look for Convenience Items	●	◐	◐	●	◐
13. Don't Support Football	⊙	⊙	●	●	◐
14. Cut Transportation Costs	◐	⊙	◐	●	◐
15. Buy Your Books Early	⊙	⊙	◐	●	●
16. Join a Cooperative	⊙	⊙	⊙	●	◐
17. Buying Technology through the College	◐	◐	⊙	◐	◐
18. Consider Earning a Dual Degree	●	●	◐	◐	●
19. Earn a Certificate in a Career Field	◐	●	●	●	●
20. Design a Transfer Plan	●	●	●	●	●

	Above Average ●	Average ◐	Below Average ⊙	Savings	Improvement to General Value	Availability	Chance of Qualifying	Impact on Long term Results
21. Select the Right College for You				●	●	●	●	●
22. Pick the Appropriate Field of Study				◐	●	●	●	●
23. Select a Major before You Start				◐	◐	●	●	●
24. Establish Career Goals Early				◐	◐	●	●	●
25. Time to Graduation				●	◐	◐	●	●
26. Take Advanced Placement Courses				◐	●	◐	◐	●
27. Attend School Year-Round				◐	◐	◐	●	●
28. Academic Calendars				●	⊙	◐	●	◐
29. Course Load				◐	⊙	●	●	◐
30. Look for Tuition Discounts				◐	◐	●	●	◐
31. Negotiate Your Aid Package				◐	◐	●	◐	◐
32. Collect a Federal Grant				●	⊙	●	●	◐
33. Get a Federal Supplement Grant				⊙	⊙	⊙	⊙	◐

	Above Average ●	Average ◐	Below Average ⊙	Savings	Improvement to General Value	Availability	Chance of Qualifying	Impact on Long term Results
34. Earn a State Grant				●	⊙	◐	●	◐
35. Take Out a Federally Subsidized Interest Loan				◐	⊙	●	●	◐
36. Take Out an Unsubsidized Interest Loan				⊙	⊙	●	●	◐
37. Use the PLUS Loan for Parents				⊙	⊙	●	●	◐
38. Look into College Work Study (CWS)				◐	⊙	◐	⊙	◐
39. Benefit from Your Financial Aid Status				◐	⊙	⊙	◐	◐
40. Delay Taking Income to Increase Aid				◐	⊙	●	◐	◐
41. Earn Institutional Scholarships for Achievement				●	◐	◐	◐	●
42. Earn a National Merit Scholarship™				●	●	⊙	⊙	●
43. Earn a State Scholarship for Academic Achievement				◐	●	⊙	⊙	●
44. Earn an Athletic Scholarship				●	⊙	⊙	⊙	◐

Legend: ● Above Average　◐ Average　◉ Below Average

	Savings	Improvement to General Value	Availability	Chance of Qualifying	Impact on Long term Results
45. Design an Asset Allocation Strategy	◐	◉	●	●	◐
46. Investigate the Hope Tax Credit	◐	◉	●	●	◐
47. Take a Lifetime Learning Tax Credit	◐	◉	●	●	◐
48. Deduct Educational Loan Interest	◐	◉	●	●	◐
49. Check Out the New Education IRAs	◐	◉	●	●	◐
50. Save Now for College Later	◐	◉	●	●	◐
51. Buy U.S. Savings Bonds	◐	◉	●	●	◐
52. Lock-in Tuition Rates with Prepaid Tuition Plans (Section 529)	◉	◉	●	●	◐
53. Discover State Sponsored "529" Investment Plans	◐	◉	●	●	◐
54. Investigate State College Savings Bonds	◐	◉	●	●	◐
55. Find a Company That Will Pay Your Tuition	●	◐	◐	◐	●

Above Average ●	Average ◐	Below Average ◉	Savings	Improvement to General Value	Availability	Chance of Qualifying	Impact on Long term Results
56. Find Work at a College			●	◉	◐	◐	◐
57. Attend a Bible College			●	◉	◉	●	◉
58. Establish State Residency			●	◐	◉	◐	◐
59. Check for Extended Billing Options			◉	◉	●	●	◐
60. Plan for Student Loan Forgiveness			●	◐	◐	●	◐
61. Become a Resident Advisor			●	◉	◐	◐	◐
62. Work While in College			◐	◐	●	●	●
63. Group Discounts			◉	◉	◉	◉	◐
64. Earn Student Discounts			◉	◉	◉	●	◐
65. Join the Armed Forces and Go to College			●	◐	◐	●	●
66. Collect the G.I. Bill			●	◐	◐	●	◐
67. Join ROTC			●	◐	◐	●	◐
68. Remember Who Pays Your Tuition			◐	◐	●	●	◐

Above Average ● / Average ◐ / Below Average ◉	Savings	Improvement to General Value	Availability	Chance of Qualifying	Impact on Long term Results
69. Education for Tomorrow	●	●	◐	●	●
70. Seek Outcomes	◐	●	◐	●	◐
71. Attend a Very Good Public University	◐	●	●	●	●
72. Avoid Party Schools	◉	◐	●	●	◐
73. Seek Out Regional Accreditation	●	●	●	●	●
74. Match Your Learning Style	◐	●	●	●	●
75. Investigate Support Services	◉	◐	◐	●	◐
76. Avoid Education Scams	◐	●	●	●	●
77. Be Cautious of Distance Learning	◐	◐	●	●	◐
78. Demand a Technology-Based Library	◐	◐	◐	●	◐
79. Look for a Technology-Centered Education	●	●	◉	●	◐
80. Find a Campus Convenient to Your Lifestyle	●	◉	●	●	◐

Above Average ● Average ◐ Below Average ◉	Savings	Improvement to General Value	Availability	Chance of Qualifying	Impact on Long term Results
81. Design Your Own Curriculum	●	●	◉	◐	●
82. Select Practitioner-Based Education	●	●	◐	●	●
83. Transfer in the Off-Quarter for Easier Admission	◐	●	◐	●	◐
84. Go to the Head of the Class	●	●	●	●	◐
85. Slide in the Back Door	●	●	◐	◐	●
86. Earn Admission to One of the Most Prestigious Private Universities	●	●	◉	◉	●
87. Consider the Top Public Universities	●	●	◉	◉	●
88. Study Abroad	◉	●	◐	◐	●
89. Review the College Mission	◉	◐	●	●	◐
90. Attend School in a City	◐	◐	◐	●	●
91. Compare Possible Major Choices	◐	◐	●	●	●
92. Meet Employers' Needs	●	●	●	●	●

Above Average ● Average ◐ Below Average ◉	Savings	Improvement to General Value	Availability	Chance of Qualifying	Impact on Long term Results
93. Build an Alumni Network	◐	◐	◉	●	●
94. Gain Work Experience	◐	◐	◐	●	●
95. Complete an Internship	●	●	◐	●	●
96. Look for a Diverse Study Body	◐	◐	◉	●	◐
97. Select a Major Based on Your Career Plans	●	◐	◐	●	●
98. Number of Students Enrolled in Your Major	◐	●	●	◐	●
99. Interdisciplinary Studies: Combined Degree Programs	◉	◐	◐	●	◐
100. Evaluate Your Chances of Getting into Professional Schools	◐	◐	◐	◐	◐

MAJOR SELECTION WORKSHEET

Name of Major:

▶ Why are you interested in this major?

_____

_____

_____

▶ Potential career fields commonly entered through this major:

- _____
- _____
- _____

▶ Current job market for these career fields:

☐ Better than Average   ☐ Average   ☐ Below Average

▶ Long term income potential:

| ☐ Exceeds your Expectations | ☐ Meets your Expectations | ☐ Is Below your Expectations |

▶ Type of college offering this major:

_____

_____

▶ How well do your abilities match the required coursework in this major:

☐ Perfect match   ☐ Okay match   ☐ Poor Match

▶ How well do your current interests match the coursework in this major:

☐ Perfect match   ☐ Okay match   ☐ Poor Match

MAJOR SELECTION WORKSHEET

Name of Major:

▶ Why are you interested in this major?

_____

_____

_____

▶ Potential career fields commonly entered through this major:

- _____

- _____

- _____

▶ Current job market for these career fields:

☐ Better than Average ☐ Average ☐ Below Average

▶ Long term income potential:

☐ Exceeds your ☐ Meets your ☐ Is Below your
  Expectations   Expectations   Expectations

▶ Type of college offering this major:

_____

_____

▶ How well do your abilities match the required coursework in this major:

☐ Perfect match ☐ Okay match ☐ Poor Match

▶ How well do your current interests match the coursework in this major:

☐ Perfect match ☐ Okay match ☐ Poor Match

MAJOR SELECTION WORKSHEET

Name of Major:

▶ Why are you interested in this major?

_____

_____

_____

▶ Potential career fields commonly entered through this major:

- _____
- _____
- _____

▶ Current job market for these career fields:

☐ Better than Average ☐ Average ☐ Below Average

▶ Long term income potential:

☐ Exceeds your ☐ Meets your ☐ Is Below your
Expectations Expectations Expectations

▶ Type of college offering this major:

_____

_____

▶ How well do your abilities match the required coursework in this major:

☐ Perfect match ☐ Okay match ☐ Poor Match

▶ How well do your current interests match the coursework in this major:

☐ Perfect match ☐ Okay match ☐ Poor Match

MAJOR SELECTION WORKSHEET

Name of Major:

▶ Why are you interested in this major?

_____

_____

_____

▶ Potential career fields commonly entered through this major:

- _____

- _____

- _____

▶ Current job market for these career fields:

☐ Better than Average   ☐ Average   ☐ Below Average

▶ Long term income potential:

☐ Exceeds your   ☐ Meets your   ☐ Is Below your
   Expectations   Expectations   Expectations

▶ Type of college offering this major:

_____

_____

▶ How well do your abilities match the required coursework in this major:

☐ Perfect match   ☐ Okay match   ☐ Poor Match

▶ How well do your current interests match the coursework in this major:

☐ Perfect match   ☐ Okay match   ☐ Poor Match

College Name:

Type of College:

Undergraduate Student Body Size:

Annual Tuition:

▶ Availability of your major choice:

☐ Offers your top 2 major choices

☐ Offers your top major choice only

☐ Does not offer your major choices

▶ Technology resources available:

☐ Above average

☐ Average

☐ Below Average

▶ Cost after average financial aid awards:

☐ Easy to meet

☐ Affordable

☐ Difficult to meet

▶ Campus atmosphere:

☐ Good fit

☐ Okay fit

☐ Poor fit

▶ Average time to graduation:

☐ Longer than 5 years

☐ 4 to 5 years

☐ Under 4 years

▶ Percent of freshmen that return for sophomore year:

- ☐ Over 90%
- ☐ 70–90%
- ☐ Below 70%

▶ College arranged internships:

- ☐ Many available
- ☐ Few available
- ☐ None available

▶ College reputation in your community:

- ☐ One of the best
- ☐ Average
- ☐ Below average

COLLEGE VISIT WORKSHEET

College Name:

Type of College:

Undergraduate Student Body Size:

Annual Tuition:

▶ Availability of your major choice:

- ☐ Offers your top 2 major choices
- ☐ Offers your top major choice only
- ☐ Does not offer your major choices

▶ Technology resources available:

- ☐ Above average
- ☐ Average
- ☐ Below Average

▶ Cost after average financial aid awards:

- ☐ Easy to meet
- ☐ Affordable
- ☐ Difficult to meet

▶ Campus atmosphere:

- ☐ Good fit
- ☐ Okay fit
- ☐ Poor fit

▶ Average time to graduation:

- ☐ Longer than 5 years
- ☐ 4 to 5 years
- ☐ Under 4 years

▶ Percent of freshmen that return for sophomore year:

- ☐ Over 90%
- ☐ 70–90%
- ☐ Below 70%

▶ College arranged internships:

- ☐ Many available
- ☐ Few available
- ☐ None available

▶ College reputation in your community:

- ☐ One of the best
- ☐ Average
- ☐ Below average

COLLEGE VISIT WORKSHEET

College Name:

Type of College:
Undergraduate Student Body Size:
Annual Tuition:

▶ Availability of your major choice:

- ☐ Offers your top 2 major choices
- ☐ Offers your top major choice only
- ☐ Does not offer your major choices

▶ Technology resources available:

- ☐ Above average
- ☐ Average
- ☐ Below Average

▶ Cost after average financial aid awards:

- ☐ Easy to meet
- ☐ Affordable
- ☐ Difficult to meet

▶ Campus atmosphere:

- ☐ Good fit
- ☐ Okay fit
- ☐ Poor fit

▶ Average time to graduation:

- ☐ Longer than 5 years
- ☐ 4 to 5 years
- ☐ Under 4 years

▶ Percent of freshmen that return for sophomore year:

- ☐ Over 90%
- ☐ 70–90%
- ☐ Below 70%

▶ College arranged internships:

- ☐ Many available
- ☐ Few available
- ☐ None available

▶ College reputation in your community:

- ☐ One of the best
- ☐ Average
- ☐ Below average

COLLEGE VISIT WORKSHEET

College Name:

Type of College:

Undergraduate Student Body Size:

Annual Tuition:

▶ Availability of your major choice:

  ☐ Offers your top 2 major choices

  ☐ Offers your top major choice only

  ☐ Does not offer your major choices

▶ Technology resources available:

  ☐ Above average

  ☐ Average

  ☐ Below Average

▶ Cost after average financial aid awards:

  ☐ Easy to meet

  ☐ Affordable

  ☐ Difficult to meet

▶ Campus atmosphere:

  ☐ Good fit

  ☐ Okay fit

  ☐ Poor fit

▶ Average time to graduation:

  ☐ Longer than 5 years

  ☐ 4 to 5 years

  ☐ Under 4 years

▶ Percent of freshmen that return for sophomore year:

☐ Over 90%

☐ 70–90%

☐ Below 70%

▶ College arranged internships:

☐ Many available

☐ Few available

☐ None available

▶ College reputation in your community:

☐ One of the best

☐ Average

☐ Below average

Index of Colleges and Universities

Adelphi University
1 South Avenue
Garden City, NY 11530-4299
Telephone: 516-877-3000
www.adelphi.edu

Adrian College
110 South Madison Street
Adrian, MI 49221-2575
Telephone: 517-265-5161
www.adrian.edu

Alabama State University
915 South Jackson Street
Montgomery, AL 36101-0271
Telephone: 334-229-4200
www.alasu.edu

Albion College
Albion, MI 49224-1899
Telephone: 517-629-1000
www.albion.edu

American Baptist College
1800 Baptist World Center Drive
Nashville, TN 37207
Telephone: 615-228-7877
www.abcnash.edu

American University
4400 Massachusetts Avenue NW
Washington, DC 20016-8003
Telephone: 202-885-1000
www.american.edu

Amherst College
P.O. Box 5000
Amherst, MA 01002-5000
Telephone: 413-542-2000
www.amherst.edu

Arizona State University
P.O. Box 872803
Tempe, AZ 85287-2803
Telephone: 480-965-9011
www.asu.edu

Arlington Baptist College
3001 West Division
Arlington, TX 76012-3497
Telephone: 817-461-8741
www.abconline.edu

Art Institute of Southern California
2222 Laguna Canyon Road
Laguna Beach, CA 92651-1136
Telephone: 949-376-6000
www.aisc.edu

Auburn University
Auburn, AL 36849-3501
Telephone: 334-844-4000
www.auburn.edu

Audrey Cohen College
75 Varick Street
New York, NY 10013-1919
Telephone: 212-343-1234
www.audrey-cohen.edu

Augustana College
639-38th Street
Rock Island, IL 61201-2296
Telephone: 309-794-7000
www.augustana.edu

Ball State University
2000 West University Avenue
Muncie, IN 47306-1099
Telephone: 765-289-1241
www.bsu.edu

Bank Street College
610 West 112st
New York, NY 10025-1898
Telephone: 212-875-4400
www.bankstreet.edu

Barnard College
3009 Broadway
New York, NY 10027-6598
Telephone: 212-854-5262
www.barnard.columbia.edu

Barry University
11300 NE Second Avenue
Miami Shores, FL 33161-6695
Telephone: 305-899-3000
www.barry.edu

Bates College
Lewistown, ME 04240-6047
Telephone: 207-786-6255
www.bates.edu

Bentley College
175 Forest Street
Waltham, MA 02452-4705
Telephone: 781-891-2000
www.bentley.edu

Beulah Heights Bible College
892 Berne Street SE
P.O. Box 18145
Atlanta, GA 30316-1873
Telephone: 770-394-8300
www.beulah.edu

Boise Bible College
8695 West Marigold Street
Boise, ID 83714-1220
Telephone: 208-376-7731
www.boisebible.edu

Boston College
140 Commonwealth Avenue
Chestnut Hill, MA 02467-3934
Telephone: 617-552-8000
www.bc.edu

Boston University
Boston, MA 02215-1700
Telephone: 617-353-2000
www.bu.edu

Bowdoin College
5000 College Station
Brunswick, ME 04011-8448
Telephone: 207-725-3000
www.bowdoin.edu

Bowling Green State University
Bowling Green, OH 43403-0001
Telephone: 419-372-2531
www.bgsu.edu

Bradley University
1501 West Bradley Avenue
Peoria, IL 61625-0001
Telephone: 309-676-7611
www.bradley.edu

Brandeis University
South Street
Waltham, MA 02254-9110
Telephone: 781-736-2000
www.brandeis.edu

Brigham Young University
Provo, UT 84602-0002
Telephone: 801-378-1211
www.byu.edu

Case Western Reserve University
10900 Euclid Avenue
Cleveland, OH 44106-7001
Telephone: 216-368-2000
www.cwru.edu

Catholic University of America
620 Michigan Avenue NE
Washington, DC 20064-0002
Telephone: 202-319-5000
www.cua.edu

Central Missouri State University
Warrensburg, MO 64093-8888
Telephone: 660-543-4111
www.cmsu.edu

Centre College
600 West Walnut Street
Danville, KY 40422-1394
Telephone: 859-238-5200
www.centre.edu

Chaminade University of Honolulu
3140 Waialae Avenue
Honolulu, HI 96816-1578
Telephone: 808-735-4711
www.chaminade.edu

Champlain College
163 South Willard Street
Burlington, VT 05402-0670
Telephone: 802-860-2700
www.champlain.edu

Chicago State University
9501 South King Drive
Chicago, IL 60628-1598
Telephone: 773-995-2000
www.csu.edu

City University
11900 NE First Street
Belluve, WA 98004
Telephone: 425-637-1010
www.cityu.edu

City University of New York (CUNY)
535 East 80th Street
New York, NY 10021-0795
Telephone: 212-794-5555
www.cuny.edu

Clark University
950 Main Street
Worcester, MA 01610-1477
Telephone: 508-793-7711
www.clarku.edu

Clarkson University
Potsdam, NY 13699-5557
Telephone: 315-268-6400
www.clarkson.edu

Clear Creek Baptist Bible College
300 Clear Creek Road
Pineville, KY 40977-9754
Telephone: 606-337-3196
www.ccbbc.edu

Cleary College
3601 Plymouth Road
Ann Arbor, MI 48105
Telephone: 734-332-4477
www.cleary.edu

Clemson University
201 Sikes Hall
Clemson, SC 29634-0001
Telephone: 864-656-3311
www.clemson.edu

Cleveland State University
E. 24th and Euclid Avenue
Cleveland, OH 44115-2440
Telephone: 216-687-2000
www.csuohio.edu/irraa

Coe College
1220 1st Avenue
Ceder Rapids, IA 52402-5092
Telephone: 319-399-8000
www.coe.edu

Columbia University
116 Street and Broadway
New York, NY 10027
Telephone: 212-854-1754
www.columbia.edu

Connecticut College
270 Mohegan Avenue
New London, CT 06320-4125
Telephone: 860-447-1911
www.connecticutcollege.edu

Cooper Union College
30 Cooper Square
New York, NY 10003-7120
Telephone: 212-353-4100
www.cooper.edu

Cornell College
600 First Street West
Mount Vernon, IA 52314-1098
Telephone: 319-895-4000
www.cornellcollege.edu

Cornell University
Ithaca, NY 14853-2801
Telephone: 607-255-2000
www.cornell.edu

Creighton University
2500 California Plaza
Omaha, NE 68178-0001
Telephone: 402-280-2700
www.creighton.edu

CUNY-Baruch College
17 Lexington Avenue
New York, NY 10010-5526
Telephone: 212-802-2000
www.baruch.cuny.edu

CUNY-Borough of Manhattan Community College
199 Chambers Street
New York, NY 10007-1047
Telephone: 212-346-8800
www.bmcc.cuny.edu

CUNY-Bronx Community College
West 181 Street & University Avenue
Bronx, NY 10453-2895
Telephone: 718-289-5100
www.cuny.edu/about_cuny/bronx.html

CUNY-Brooklyn College
2900 Bedford Avenue
Brooklyn, NY 11210-2889
Telephone: 718-951-5000
www.brooklyn.cuny.edu

CUNY-City College
138 Convent Avenue
New York, NY 10031-9198
Telephone: 212-650-7000
www.ccny.cuny.edu

CUNY-College of Staten Island
2800 Victory Boulevard
Staten Island, NY 10314-6600
Telephone: 718-982-2000
www.csi.cuny.edu

CUNY-Graduate School and University Center
365 Fifth Avenue
New York, NY 10016-4309
Telephone: 212-817-7000
www.gc.cuny.edu

CUNY-Hostos Community College
500 Grand Concourse
Bronx, NY 10451-5323
Telephone: 718-518-4300
www.hostos.cuny.edu

CUNY-Hunter College
695 Park Avenue
New York, NY 10021-5085
Telephone: 212-772-4000
www.hunter.cuny.edu

Dickinson College
College & Louther Street
P.O. Box 1773
Carlisle, PA 17013-2896
Telephone: 717-243-5121
www.dickinson.edu

Drake University
2507 University Avenue
Des Moines, IA 50311-4505
Telephone: 515-271-2011
www.drake.edu

Drew University
36 Madison Avenue
Madison, NJ 07940-1493
Telephone: 973-408-3000
www.drew.edu

Duke University
Durham, NC 27706-8001
Telephone: 919-684-8111
www.duke.edu

Earlham College
801 National Road West
Richmond, IN 47374-4095
Telephone: 765-983-1200
www.earlham.edu

East Central University
Ada, OK 74820-6899
Telephone: 580-332-8000
www.ecok.edu

Eastern Iowa Community College
306 West River Drive
Davenport, IA 52801-1221
Telephone: 563-336-3300
www.easterniowa.org

Emerson College
120 Boylston Street
Boston, MA 02116-1596
Telephone: 617-824-8500
www.emerson.edu

Emory University
Atlanta, GA 30322-0001
Telephone: 404-627-2681
www.emory.edu

Erskine College
P.O. Box 338
Due West, SC 29639-0338
Telephone: 864-379-2131
www.erskine.edu

Fairfield University
1073 North Benson Road
Fairfield, CT 06430-5195
Telephone: 203-254-4000
www.fairfield.edu

Fairleigh Dickenson University
1000 River Road
Teaneck, NJ 07666-1996
Telephone: 201-692-2000
www.fdu.edu

Faith Baptist Bible College
1900 Northwest 4th Street
Ankeny, IA 50021-2152
Telephone: 515-964-0601
www.faith.edu

Fitchburg State College
160 Pearl Street
Fitchburg, MA 01420-2697
Telephone: 978-345-2151
www.fsc.edu

Florida State University
Tallahassee, FL 32306-9936
Telephone: 850-644-2525
www.fsu.edu

Fordham University
East Fordham Road
Bronx, NY 10458-9993
Telephone: 718-817-1000
www.fordham.edu

Hanover College
P.O. Box 108
Hanover, IN 47243-0108
Telephone: 812-866-7000
www.hanover.edu

Harrisburg Area Community College
1 HACC Drive
Harrisburg, PA 17110-2999
Telephone: 717-780-2300
www.hacc.edu

Harvard University
Cambridge, MA 02138-3800
Telephone: 617-495-1000
www.harvard.edu

Harvey Mudd College
301 East 12th Street
Claremont, CA 91711-5994
Telephone: 909-621-8000
www.hmc.edu

Hawaii Pacific University
1164 Bishop Street
Honolulu, HI 96813-2882
Telephone: 808-544-0200
www.hpu.edu

Heritage Christian University
P.O. Box HCU
Florence, AL 35630
Telephone: 205-766-6610
www.hcu.edu

Heritage College
3240 Fort Road
Toppenish, WA 98948-9599
Telephone: 509-865-8500
www.heritage.edu

Hillsdale College
33 East College
Hillsdale, MI 49242-1298
Telephone: 517-437-7341
www.hillsdale.edu

Hobe Sound Bible College
P.O. Box 1065
Hobe Sound, FL 33475-1065
Telephone: 561-546-5534
www.hsbc.edu

Hocking Technical College
3301 Hocking Parkway
Nelsonville, OH 45764-9704
Telephone: 740-753-3591
www.hocking.edu

Holy Family College
Grant & Frankford Avenues
Philadelphia, PA 19114-2094
Telephone: 215-637-7700
www.hfc.edu

Houston Baptist University
7502 Fondren Road
Houston, TX 77074-3298
Telephone: 281-649-3000
www.hbu.edu

Howard University
2400 Sixth Street NW
Washington, DC 20059-0001
Telephone: 202-806-6100
www.howard.edu

Idaho State University
921 South 8th
Pocatello, ID 83209-0009
Telephone: 208-282-0211
www.isu.edu

Illinois Institute of Technology
3300 South Federal Street
Chicago, IL 60616-3793
Telephone: 312-567-3000
www.iit.edu

Illinois State University
School and North Streets
Normal, IL 61790-0001
Telephone: 309-438-2111
www.ilstu.edu

Kent State University
P.O Box 5190
Kent, OH 44242-0001
Telephone: 330-672-2121
www.kent.edu

Kent State University
Geauga Campus
14111 Claridon Troy Road
Burton Township, OH 44021-9500
Telephone: 440-834-4187
www.geauga.kent.edu

Kenyon College
Gambier, OH 43022-9623
Telephone: 740-427-5000
www.kenyon.edu

Knox College
2 East South Street
Galesburg, IL 61401-4999
Telephone: 309-341-7000
www.knox.edu

Lafayette College
Easton, PA 18042-1798
Telephone: 610-330-5000
www.lafayette.edu

Lake Forest College
555 North Sheridan Road
Lake Forest, IL 60045-2399
Telephone: 847-234-3100
www.lfc.edu

Lakeland College
P.O. Box 359
Sheboygan, WI 53082-0359
Telephone: 920-565-2111
www.lakeland.edu

Lamar University
211 Redbird Lane
Beaumont, TX 77710
Telephone: 409-880-7011
www.lamar.edu

LaSalle University
1900 West Onley
Philadelphia, PA 19141-1199
Telephone: 215-951-1000
www.lasalle.edu

LeHigh University
27 Memorial Drive West
Bethelehem, PA 18015-3094
Telephone: 610-758-3000
www.lehigh.edu

LeMoyne College
1419 Salt Springs Road
Syracuse, NY 13214-1399
Telephone: 315-445-4400
www.lemoyne.edu

Lewis & Clark College
615 South West Palatine Hill Road
Portland, OR 97219-7899
Telephone: 503-768-7000
www.lclark.edu

Lewis University
5003 Independence Blvd.
Romeoville, IL 60446-2298
Telephone: 815-838-0500
www.lewisu.edu

Liberty University
1971 University Blvd.
Lynchburg, VA 24502-2269
Telephone: 434-582-2000
www.liberty.edu

Lincoln University
401 15th Street
Oakland, CA 94612-2801
Telephone: 510-628-8010
www.lincolnuca.edu

Lincoln University
Jefferson City, MO 65102-0029
Telephone: 573-681-5000
www.lincolnu.edu

Michigan State University
East Lansing, MI 48824-1046
Telephone: 517-355-1855
www.msu.edu

Middle Tennessee State University
Murfreesboro, TN 37132-0001
Telephone: 615-898-2300
www.mtsu.edu

Middlebury College
Middlebury, VT 05753-6200
Telephone: 802-443-5000
www.middlebury.edu

Millikan University
1184 West Main Street
Decatur, IL 62522-2084
Telephone: 217-424-6211
www.millikin.edu

Millsaps College
Jackson, MS 39210-0001
Telephone: 601-974-1000
www.millsaps.edu

Minnesota Bible College
920 Mayowood Road SW
Rochester, MN 55902-2382
Telephone: 507-288-4563
www.mnbc.edu

Mississippi State University
Mississippi State, MS 39762-5708
Telephone: 662-325-2323
www.msstate.edu

Mississippi Valley State University
Itta Bena, MS 38941-1400
Telephone: 601-254-9041
www.mvsu.edu

Montana State University
P.O. Box 172000
Bozeman, MT 59717-2000
Telephone: 406-994-0211
www.montana.edu

Montclair State University
Upper Montclair, NJ 07043-9987
Telephone: 973-655-4000
www.montclair.edu

Moody Bible Institute
820 North Lasalle Boulevard
Chicago, IL 60610-3263
Telephone: 312-329-4000
www.moody.edu

Morehouse College
830 Westview Drive SW
Atlanta, GA 30314-3773
Telephone: 404-681-2800
www.morehouse.edu

Murray State University
P.O. Box 9
Murray, KY 42071-0009
Telephone: 270-762-3011
www.murraystate.edu

National University
11255 North Torrey Pines Road
La Jolla, CA 92037-1011
Telephone: 858-563-7100
www.nu.edu

National-Louis University
2840 Sheridan Road
Evanston, IL 60201-1796
Telephone: 847-475-1100
www.nl.edu

Nazarene Bible College
1111 Academy Park Loop
Colorado Springs, CO 80910-3704
Telephone: 719-884-5000
www.nbc.edu

Nazarene Indian Bible College
2315 Markham Road SW
Albequerque, NM 87105
Telephone: 505-877-0240
www.nibc.net

Ohio State University - Columbus
Columbus, OH 43210-1358
Telephone: 614-292-6446
www.osu.edu

Ohio University
Athens, OH 45701-2979
Telephone: 740-593-1000
www.ohiou.edu

Ohio Wesleyan University
61 South Sandusky Street
Delaware, OH 43015-2598
Telephone: 740-368-2000
www.owu.edu

Oklahoma Baptist University
500 West University
Shawnee, OK 74804-2590
Telephone: 405-275-2850
www.okbu.edu

Oklahoma State University
301 Whitehurst
Stillwater, OK 74078-1025
Telephone: 405-744-5000
www.okstate.edu

Old Dominion University
5115 Hampton Blvd.
Norfolk, VA 23529-1000
Telephone: 757-683-3000
www.odu.edu

Oral Roberts University
7777 South Lewis
Tulsa, OK 74171-0003
Telephone: 981-495-6161
www.oru.edu

Oregon State University
Corvallis, OR 97331-8507
Telephone: 541-737-0123
www.orst.edu

Our Lady of Holy Cross College
4123 Woodland Drive
New Orleans, LA 70131-7399
Telephone: 504-394-7744
www.olhcc.edu

Pace University
1 Pace Plaza
New York, NY 10038-1598
Telephone: 212-346-1200
www.pace.edu

Penn State -University Park
201 Old Main
University Park, PA 16802-1589
Telephone: 814-865-4700
www.psu.edu

Pepperdine University
24255 Pacific Coast Highway
Malibu, CA 90263-0001
Telephone: 310-506-4000
www.pepperdine.edu

Portland State University
P.O. Box 751
Portland, OR 97207-0751
Telephone: 503-725-3000
www.pdx.edu

Practical Bible College
400 Riverside Drive
Johnson City, NY 13790
Telephone: 607-729-1581
www.practical.edu

Prescott College
220 Grove Avenue
Prescott, AZ 86301-2990
Telephone: 520-778-2090
www.prescott.edu

Princeton University
Princeton, NJ 08544-1098
Telephone: 609-258-3000
www.princeton.edu

San Jose Christian College
790 S. 12th Street
San Jose, CA 95112-2381
Telephone: 408-278-4300
www.sjchristian.edu

San Jose State University
One Washington Square
San Jose, CA 95192-0001
Telephone: 408-924-1000
www.sjsu.edu

Santa Clara University
Santa Clara, CA 95053-0001
Telephone: 408-554-4000
www.scu.edu

**School of the Art Institute
of Chicago**
37 South Wabash
Chicago, IL 60603-3103
Telephone: 312-899-5100
www.artic.edu/saic/saichome.html

Selma University
1501 Lapsley Street
Selma, AL 36701
Telephone: 334-872-2533

Seton Hall University
400 South Orange Avenue
South Orange, NJ 07079-2697
Telephone: 973-761-9000
www.shu.edu

Siena College
515 London Road
Loudonville, NY 12211-1462
Telephone: 518-783-2300
www.siena.edu

Skidmore College
815 North Broadway
Saratoga Springs, NY 12866-1632
Telephone: 518-580-5000
www.skidmore.edu

Smith College
Northampton, MA 01063-0001
Telephone: 413-584-2700
www.smith.edu

Southeastern University
501 I Street SW
Washington, DC 20024-2788
Telephone: 202-488-8162
www.seu.edu

**Southern Arkansas
University Tech**
100 Carr Road
Camden, AR 71701-4648
Telephone: 870-574-4500
www.sautech.edu

Southern Illinois University
Stone Center
Carbondale, IL 62901-6801
Telephone: 618-536-3331
www.siu.edu

**Southern Methodist
University**
6425 Boaz Street
P.O. Box 100
Dallas, TX 75275-0001
Telephone: 214-768-2000
www.smu.edu

**Southern University-
New Orleans**
6400 Press Drive
New Orleans, LA 70126-0002
Telephone: 504-286-5000
www.suno.edu

Southwestern College
2625 East Cactus Road
Phoenix, AZ 85032-7042
Telephone: 602-992-6101
www.southwesterncollege.edu

St. Olaf College
1520 St. Olaf Avenue
Northfield, MN 55057-1098
Telephone: 507-646-2222
www.stolaf.com

St. Peter's College
2641 Kennedy Boulevard
Jersey City, NJ 07306-5997
Telephone: 201-915-9000
www.spc.edu

Stanford University
Stanford, CA 94305-1684
Telephone: 650-723-2300
www.stanford.edu

State University of New York (SUNY)
State University Plaza
New York, NY 12246-0001
Telephone: 518-443-5555
www.suny.edu

Stillman College
3600 Stillman Blvd
P.O. Box 1430
Tuscaloosa, AL 35403-1430
Telephone: 205-349-4240
www.stillman.edu

SUNY College of Agriculture and Technology-Morrisville
Morrisville, NY 13408-0636
Telephone: 315-684-6000
www.morrisville.edu

SUNY College of Environment Science
One Forestry Drive
Syracuse, NY 13210-2778
Telephone: 315-470-6500
www.esf.com

SUNY College of Optometry
33 West 42nd Street
New York, NY 10036-8003
Telephone: 212-780-4900
www.sunyopt.edu

SUNY College of Technology-Alfred
Alfred, NY 14802-1196
Telephone: 607-587-4111
www.alfredstate.edu

SUNY College of Technology-Canton
Canton, NY 13617-1098
Telephone: 315-336-7011
www.canton.edu

SUNY College of Technology-Delhi
Delhi, NY 13753-1190
Telephone: 607-746-4000
www.delhi.edu

SUNY College of Technology-Farmingdale
Melville Road
Farmingdale, NY 11735-1021
Telephone: 516-420-2000
www.farmingdale.edu

SUNY Health Science Center-Brooklyn
450 Clarkson Avenue
Brooklyn, NY 11203-2098
Telephone: 718-270-1000
www.downstate.edu

SUNY Institute of Technology-Utica/Rome
Marcy Campus
P.O. Box 3050
Utica, NY 13504-3050
Telephone: 315-464-5540
www.sunyid.edu

SUNY-Potsdam
Pierrepont Avenue
Potsdam, NY 13676-2294
Telephone: 315-267-2000
www.potsdam.edu

SUNY-Purchase
Purshase, NY 10577-1400
Telephone: 914-251-6000
www.purchase.edu

SUNY-Stony Brook
Stony Brook, NY 11794-0001
Telephone: 516-689-6000
www.sunysb.edu

**SUNY-Ulster County
Community College**
Stone Ridge, NY 12484
Telephone: 845-687-5000
www.ulster.cc.ny.edu

**SUNY-Westchester
Community College**
75 Grassland Road
Valhalla, NY 10595-1636
Telephone: 914-785-6600
www.sunywcc.edu

Swarthmore College
500 College Avenue
Swarthmore, PA 19081-1390
Telephone: 610-328-8000
www.swarthmore.edu

Syracuse University
Syracuse, NY 13244-1100
Telephone: 315-443-1870
www.syracuse.edu

**Texas A&M University-
College Station**
College Station, TX 77843-0001
Telephone: 979-845-3211
www.tamu.edu

Texas A&M-Corpus Christi
6300 Ocean Drive
Corpus Christi, TX 78412-5503
Telephone: 361-825-5700
www.tamucc.edu

The Atlanta College of Art
1280 Peachtree Street NE
Atlanta, GA 30309-3502
Telephone: 404-733-5001
www.aca.edu

The Citadel
171 Moultrie Street
Charleston, SC 29409-0001
Telephone: 843-953-5000
www.citadel.edu

Transylvania University
300 North Broadway
Lexington, KY 40508-1797
Telephone: 859-233-8300
www.transy.edu

Trinity College
300 Summit Street
Hartford, CT 06106-3100
Telephone: 860-297-2000
www.trincoll.edu

Trinity University
715 Stadium Drive
San Antonio, TX 78212-7200
Telephone: 210-999-7011
www.trinity.edu

Troy State University-Montgomery
231 Montgomery Street
P.O. Box 4419
Mongomery, AL 36104-4419
Telephone: 334-834-1400
www.tsum.edu

Tufts University
Medford, MA 02155-5555
Telephone: 617-628-5000
www.tufts.edu

University of California-Berkeley
Berkeley, CA 94720-0001
Telephone: 510-642-6000
www.berkeley.edu

University of California-Irvine
Campus Drive
Irvine, CA 92697-0001
Telephone: 949-824-5011
www.uci.edu

University of California-Los Angeles
405 Hilgard Avenue
Los Angeles, CA 90095-1405
Telephone: 310-825-4321
www.ucla.edu

University of California-Santa Barbara
Santa Barbara, CA 93106
Telephone: 805-893-8000
www.ucsb.edu

University of Chicago
5801 South Ellis Avenue
Chicago, IL 60637-1496
Telephone: 773-702-1234
www.uchicago.edu

University of Cincinatti
2624 Clifton Avenue
Cincinnati, OH 45221
Telephone: 513-556-6000
www.uc.edu

University of Colorado-Boulder
Boulder, CO 80309-0001
Telephone: 303-492-1411
www.colorado.edu

University of Colorado-Denver
P.O. Box 173364
Denver, CO 80217-3364
Telephone: 303-556-2400
www.cudenver.edu

University of Connecticut
Storrs, CT 06269-0001
Telephone: 860-486-2000
www.uconn.edu

University of Dallas
1845 East Northgate
Irving, TX 75062-4799
Telephone: 972-721-5000
www.udallas.edu

University of Dayton
300 College Park
Dayton, OH 45469-0001
Telephone: 937-229-1000
www.udayton.edu

University of Delaware
Newark, DE 19716
Telephone: 302-831-2000
www.udel.edu

University of Denver
University Park
Denver, CO 80208-0001
Telephone: 303-871-2000
www.du.edu

University of Detroit-Mercy
4001 West McNichols Road
Box 19900
Detroit, MI 48219-0900
Telephone: 313-993-1000
www.udmercy.edu

University of Florida
Gainsville, FL 32611-9500
Telephone: 352-392-3261
www.ufl.edu

University of Georgia
Athens, GA 30602-0001
Telephone: 706-542-3000
www.uga.edu

University of Houston
212 East Cullen Bldg.
Houston, TX 77204-2018
Telephone: 713-743-1000
www.uh.edu

University of Houston-Downtown
1 Main Street
Houston, TX 77002-1014
Telephone: 713-221-8000
www.uhd.edu

University of Illinois-Chicago
601 South Morgon-M/C 102
Chicago, IL 60607-7128
Telephone: 312-996-7000
www.uic.edu

University of Illinois-Urbana-Champaign
Urbana, IL 61801
Telephone: 217-333-1000
www.uiuc.edu

University of Iowa
Iowa City, IA 52242-0001
Telephone: 319-335-3500
www.uiowa.edu

University of Louisiana-Monroe
700 University Avenue
Monroe, LA 71209-0001
Telephone: 318-342-1000
www.nlu.edu

University of Maine-Augusta
46 University Drive
Augusta, ME 04330-9410
Telephone: 207-621-3000
www.uma.maine.edu

University of Maine-Orono
Orono, ME 04469-0001
Telephone: 207-581-1110
www.umaine.edu

University of Mary Hardin Baylor
M H-B Station
Belton, TX 76513
Telephone: 254-295-8642
www.umhb.edu

University of Maryland-Baltimore
520 West Lombard Street
Baltimore, MD 21201-1627
Telephone: 410-706-3100
www.umaryland.edu

University of Maryland-College Park
College Park, MD 20742-0001
Telephone: 301-405-1000
www.maryland.edu

University of Maryland-Eastern Shore
Princess Anne, MD 21853-1299
Telephone: 410-651-2200
www.umes.edu

University of Massachusetts-Amherst
Amherst, MA 01003-0001
Telephone: 413-545-0111
www.umasss.edu

University of Massachusetts-Boston
100 Morrissey Boulevard
Boston, MA 02125-3393
Telephone: 617-287-5000
www.umb.edu

University of Miami
140 Corniche Avenue
P.O. Box 248105
Coral Gables, FL 33146-4020
Telephone: 305-284-2211
www.miami.edu

University of Michigan-Ann Arbor
Ann Arbor, MI 48109-1318
Telephone: 734-764-1817
www.umich.edu

University of Michigan-Dearborn
4901 Evergreen Road
Dearborn, MI 48128-1491
Telephone: 313-593-5000
www.umd.umich.edu

University of Minnesota-Twin Cities
100 Church Street SE
Minneapolis, MN 55455-0213
Telephone: 612-625-5000
www1.umn.edu/tc

University of Mississippi
University, MS 38677-9999
Telephone: 662-915-7211
www.olemiss.edu

University of Missouri-Columbia
Columbia, MO 65211-0001
Telephone: 573-882-2121
www.missouri.edu

University of Nebraska
3835 Holdrege
Lincoln, NE 68583-0745
Telephone: 402-472-2111
www.uneb.edu

University of Nebraska-Lincoln
14th & R Streets
Lincoln, NE 68588-0002
Telephone: 402-472-7211
www.unl.edu

University of Nebraska-Omaha
6001 Dodge Street
Omaha, NE 68182-0001
Telephone: 402-554-2800
www.unomaha.com

University of New Hampshire
Durham, NH 03824
Telephone: 603-862-1234
www.unh.edu

University of New Orleans
Lake Front
New Orleans, LA 70148-2000
Telephone: 504-280-6000
www.uno.edu

University of North Carolina-Chapel Hill
Chapel Hill, NC 27599-0001
Telephone: 919-962-2211
www.unc.edu

University of North Carolina-Charlotte
9201 University City Boulevard
Charlotte, NC 28223-0001
Telephone: 687-687-2000
www.uncc.edu

University of North Carolina-Greensboro
P.O. Box 26170
Greensboro, NC 27402-6170
Telephone: 336-334-5000
www.uncg.edu

University of North Carolina-Pembroke
One University Drive
P.O. Box 1510
Pembroke, NC 28372-1510
Telephone: 910-521-6000
www.uncp.edu

University of Notre Dame
Notre Dame, IN 46556
Telephone: 219-631-5000
www.nd.edu

University of Vermont
Burlington, VT 05405-0160
Telephone: 802-656-3131
www.uvm.edu

University of Virgin Islands
2 John Brewers Bay
Saint Thomas, VI 00802-9990
Telephone: 340-776-9200
www.uvi.edu

University of Virginia
Charlottesville, VA 22903
Telephone: 434-924-0311
www.virgina.edu

University of Washington
Seattle, WA 98195-0001
Telephone: 206-543-2100
www.washington.edu

University of West Alabama
Livingston, AL 35470
Telephone: 205-652-3400
www.uwa.edu

**University of Wisconsin
System**
1220 Linden Drive
Madison, WI 53706-1559
Telephone: 608-262-2321
www.wisconsin.edu

**University of Wisconsin-
Green Bay**
2420 Nicolet Drive
Green Bay, WI 54311-7001
Telephone: 920-465-2000
www.uwgb.edu

**University of Wisconsin-
Madison**
500 Lincoln Drive
Madison, WI 53706-1380
Telephone: 608-262-1234
www.wisc.edu

**University of Wisconsin-
Milwaukee**
P.O. Box 413
Milwaukee, WI 53201-0413
Telephone: 414-229-1122
www.uwm.edu

**University of Wisconsin-
Superior**
Belknap & Catlin
P.O. Box 2000
Superior, WI 54880-2898
Telephone: 715-394-8101
www.uwsuper.edu

Utah State University
Logan, UT 84322-0001
Telephone: 435-797-1000
www.usu.edu

**Valley Forge Christian
College**
1401 Charleston Road
Phoenixville, PA 19460-2399
Telephone: 610-935-0450
www.vfcc.edu

Vanderbilt University
Nashville, TN 37240-0001
Telephone: 615-322-7311
www.vanderbilt.edu

Vassar College
124 Raymond Avenue
Poughkeepsie, NY 12604
Telephone: 845-437-7000
www.vassar.edu

Vennard College
2300 8th Avenue E
P.O. Box 29
University Park, IA 52595-0029
Telephone: 515-673-8391
www.vennard.edu

Westmont College
955 La Paz Road
Santa Barbara, CA 93108-1089
Telephone: 805-565-6000
www.westmont.edu

Wheaton College
26 East Main Street
Norton, MA 02766-2322
Telephone: 508-285-7722
www.wheatonma.edu

Wichita State University
1845 North Fairmount
Wichita, KS 67260-0001
Telephone: 316-978-3456
www.wichita.edu

Widener University
One University Place
Chester, PA 19013-5792
Telephone: 610-499-4000
www.widener.edu

Willamette University
900 State Street
Salem, OR 97301-3930
Telephone: 503-370-6300
www.williamette.edu

William Jewell College
500 College Hill
Liberty, MO 64068-1896
Telephone: 816-781-7700
www.jewell.edu

Williams College
Williamstown, MA 01267
Telephone: 413-597-3131
www.williams.edu

Wilmington College
320 Dupont Highway
New Castle, DE 19720-6491
Telephone: 302-328-9401
www.wilmcoll.edu

Wright State University
3640 Colonel Glenn Highway
Dayton, OH 45435-0001
Telephone: 937-777-3333
www.wright.edu

Xavier University
Victory Parkway
Cincinnati, OH 45207-1096
Telephone: 513-745-3000
www.xu.edu

Yale University
New Haven, CT 06520
Telephone: 203-432-4771
www.yale.edu